Origins of enterprise

KATRINA HONEYMAN

Origins of enterprise

BUSINESS LEADERSHIP
IN THE INDUSTRIAL REVOLUTION

MANCHESTER UNIVERSITY PRESS

ST. MARTIN'S PRESS NEW YORK

Copyright © Katrina Honeyman 1982

Published by
Manchester University Press
Oxford Road, Manchester M13 9PL

British Library cataloguing in publication data

Honeyman, Katrina.
  Origins of enterprise: business leadership in
  the industrial revolution.
  1. Entrepreneur – History.
  2. Business enterprises – Great Britain – History.
  I. Title.
  338'.04'0941   HC255
  ISBN 0–7190–0873–5

All rights reserved. For information write:
St. Martin's Press Inc., 175 Fifth Avenue, New York, NY 10010
First published in the United States of America in 1983

Library of Congress Cataloging in Publication Data

Honeyman, Katrina.
  Origins of enterprise.

  Based on the author's thesis (Ph. D.) – University of Nottingham, 1977.
  Bibliography: p.
  Includes index.
  1. Businessmen – Great Britain – History.
  2. Great Britain – Industries – History.
  3. Entrepreneur – History – I. Title.
  HC254.5.H657   1983   338'.04'0941   82–10441
  ISBN 0–312–58848–8

Photoset in Garamond
by Northern Phototypesetting Co., Bolton
Printed in Great Britain
by Biddles Ltd, Guildford, Surrey

CONTENTS

LIST OF TABLES

ACKNOWLEDGEMENTS

This work stems from a Ph.D. thesis completed in 1977 under the supervision of Dr Stanley Chapman at the University of Nottingham. I should like to thank both him and Professor A. W. Coats for their advice in the early stages. Thanks are also due to Mr T. Wragg, Keeper of Manuscripts at Chatsworth House, for allowing me to consult the Devonshire papers, and to the many librarians and archivists, particularly Ms Freda Wilkins of the Nottingham Central Library, who gave me access to their records.

More recently a number of people have offered help and criticism, most of which I accepted. In particular I should like to thank Professor A. E. Musson, Professor P. L. Payne and Dr Leslie Hannah for their valuable advice; and my present colleague, Dr Gerard Turnbull, who has given most generously of his time and expertise.

I am grateful to the secretarial staff in the School of Economic Studies at the University of Leeds for their patience and accuracy in typing the final draft of the manuscript.

Last, but by no means least, my husband, Jordan Goodman, deserves a special mention for support and encouragement in a variety of ways.

LIST OF ABBREVIATIONS

B.C.M.L.	Bolton City Museum and Library
D.P.L.	Derby Public Library
D.R.O.	Derbyshire Record Office, Matlock
J.R.L.	John Rylands University Library of Manchester
L.J.R.O.	Lichfield Joint Record Office
L.R.O.	Lancashire Record Office, Preston
M.C.L.	Manchester Central Library
M.M.	*Manchester Mercury*
N.C.L.	Nottingham City Library
N.J.	*Nottingham Journal*
N.R.	*Nottingham Review*
O.C.	*Oldham Chronicle*
O.P.L.	Oldham Public Library
S.C.L.	Sheffield City Library
U.B.D.	*Universal British Directory of Trade, Commerce and Manufacture*

I

Introduction

The period encompassing the late eighteenth and early nineteenth centuries is generally perceived as one of change in the British economy and society. The dynamism of the economy is traditionally interpreted in terms of a shift from domestically organised industry to factory production, accompanied by the introduction of new industries, more advanced technology and a rise in productivity. Social change is typically illustrated by the development of a new scheme of class relationships,[1] and by the increase in the size and mobility, both geographical and social, of the population.

Many believe that the structure of the economy and industry experienced its first significant change for centuries at this time, and that this amounted to an 'industrial revolution'. Consequently, it is argued, unprecedented opportunities emerged for a shift in industrial leadership, permitting a transformation of the power structure. Economic change, therefore, created new opportunities; and social change, particularly the apparent easing of class rigidity, facilitated the utilisation of these opportunities by individuals of diverse origins. British society from the mid-eighteenth century was 'so flexible, the economy was growing at many different points and the need for capital and enterprise so widespread after 1760 that all sectors of society supplied the men of enterprise'.[2]

The fluid structure of many industries, particularly the new ones,[3] apparently encouraged the diversity of personnel type involved in manufacturing processes: 'investors, contrivors, industrialists and entrepreneurs (it is not easy to distinguish one from another at a period of rapid change) came from every social class and from all parts of the country',[4] and Crouzet remarks that 'the founders of "factory" industries obtained capital from diverse sources . . .'.[5]

In terms of low fixed capital requirements and of industry's receptiveness to change, the early stages of industrialisation offered the greatest opportunities for new men, and especially men of limited means, to emerge. These men were in a position to make a substantial contribution to British industry, particularly through originality of approach to manufacture and by encouraging a shift away from traditional methods. The effect on the cotton trade of the 'energetic entrepreneur who lacked capital', states Lee, 'was crucial for its development, and while their achievement must be fully recognised it was still vitally important that the structure of the cotton trade should be sufficiently flexible in the later years of the eighteenth century to benefit fully from the enterprise of these industrial pioneers'.[6]

The contribution of the small man in particular to the new industrial leadership has been stressed. Alfred Marshall once said that half the early entrepreneurs had been born in a cottage and worked their way up,[7] and Crouzet asserts that their 'origins were often humble',[8] or more specifically that the capital supplied by '. . . artisans seems to have been substantial, allowing for the fact that, at the beginning of the Industrial Revolution, the threshold of entry into factory production was relatively low'.[9]

The emergence of the small man was, in principle, made possible by the 'astonishingly small' initial capital requirements for entering 'even the most capital intensive industries',[10] minimised by the application of a variety of capital economising techniques. The partnership system 'provided . . . particularly for men of modest origin, opportunity of supplementing [their] limited capital',[11] and the practice of letting factory space to small manufacturers was commonplace.[12] Although the demands of working capital were frequently unexpectedly large, 'it was . . . possible for firms beginning in a small way and with greatly inadequate capital resources of their own to insert themselves into the circulation of credit, and in this way to acquire working capital by a process of running creditor balances of much larger amounts than debtors'.[13] Industrial enterprises during the early years of factory production typically expanded their activities gradually through the retention of profits, thus reducing any possible disadvantage to the small man, and the 'critical innovations were concentrated at first in a small sector of the economy, and their appetite for capital was correspondingly limited'.[14]

What is being stressed, therefore, is the democratisation of industry; the removal, in principle, of the established economic order and the potential weakening of the traditional power structure. Any man, even one of humble origins, might thus attain a position of power through the opportunities created by the interaction of social and economic change.

Social historians have participated in the debate by emphasising the favourable social environment from the mid-eighteenth century for the emergence of the small man equipped with the necessary values,[15] that is, a society exemplified by the entrepreneurial ideal. The new society embodied the principle of competition, in contrast to the 'monopoly', 'privilege' and 'restriction' of the old economic order, and was held to be universally beneficial. It was, above all, socially beneficial.[16] The 'theory of self-dependence', as J. S. Mill was to call it, in contrast to the theory of dependence and protection, evoked not only manly self-respect and responsibility but also the ambition to rise in social status which was said to be the chief source of the energy and drive behind the progress of society.[17] Mill believed, moreover, that industrialism had increased the individual's life chances: '. . . human beings are no longer born to their place in life . . . but are free to employ their faculties and such favourable chances as offer, to achieve the lot which may appear to them most desirable'.[18] So competition, and particularly individual competition, characterised the new society; and the entrepreneur, according to the ideal, was the lynchpin of society.[19]

Samuel Smiles, the 'authorised and pious chronicler' of the mid-nineteenth century, explicitly outlined the qualities of character necessary for success in the new industrial age,[20] and advocated social mobility through self-help. His conviction, made manifest in his writing, was that any man, however humble his roots, might acquire the requisite personality traits and thus achieve greatness in the industrial sphere, though his concept of the self-made man could, in principle, apply to any individual who had practised self-improvement and effort. '. . . [I]t is not the man of the greatest natural vigour and capacity who achieves the highest results, but he who employs his powers with the greatest industry and the most carefully disciplined skill . . . the skill that comes by labour, application and experience.'[21] Moreover, 'the greatest results in life are usually attained by simple means and the exercise of ordinary qualities . . . In pursuit of even the highest branches of human enquiring, the commoner qualities are found the most useful – such as common sense, attention, application and perseverance.'[22]

Smiles had precursors and followers: in essence, he popularised apparently widely held views. 'Some are born with fortune,' stated a contemporary, but 'more are born without any and the struggle for it is very serious. It is the best educated of these, the most talented and industrious who take the prize, but all may possess industry which is, after all, the starting point and by far the most valuable power.'[23] 'The self-made man', moreover, was believed to be 'the ideal entrepreneur, the man without any initial property or patronage, any education other than self-education, or any advantage other than native talent, who by self-help and force of character made his way to wealth and status'.[24]

Despite his collection of stories of self-made men (only a small proportion of whom prove, on examination, to have humble origins) the virtues Smiles espoused were essentially Victorian middle-class ideals, hardly applicable to the contemporary factory worker. Commentators have noted that the working man typically had little inclination to sacrifice his basic comforts, even temporarily, in order to rise up the social and economic scale. Pollard argues that, on the whole, working men were non-accumulative, non-acquisitive, accustomed to work for subsistence and not for maximisation of income.[25] The attitude of the working class in general to the advantages of self-help was one of complete indifference or hostility; they were, in effect, 'culturally resistant to the dominant values of respectable Victorian society'.[26]

Among contemporary and modern writers the view persists that in the early stages of industrialisation enterprise was provided by diverse social groups, and notably by the ambitious and determined man of humble origins. This suggests that the pattern of industrial leadership changed; in principle it was democratised. The same notion, moreover, implies a sharp break with the past and, further, that the pre-industrial economy had exhibited static features which contrasted significantly with the dynamic, flexible economy of the late eighteenth century.[27] Recent research, however, has illustrated the essential dynamism of early modern England with respect to its society and its economy.

Lawrence Stone and Franklin Mendels have independently indicated the fluidity of society through social mobility, and the latter, using his concept of proto-industrialisation, has also pointed to significant movement within the economy. From the work of Stone it becomes clear that pre-industrial society was neither uniquely open nor closed but that particularly in the period 1540–1640 there existed opportunities for upward mobility as well as possibilities for downward mobility.[28] In essence, social mobility was not something new to the eighteenth century; flexibility within society had been evident for some time previously.

These conclusions are substantiated by some recent work of Mendels in which he examines the nature of social mobility in a variety of industrial stages. In reiterating his idea that a stage of industrial production existed between the domestic and factory systems, he stresses the relationship between proto-industrialisation and upward and downward mobility. Initially, pre-industrial mobility was related to the nature of the inheritance system, but as agricultural techniques and improvements led to a more efficient use of the existing land, and industrial and service occupations opened up, the latter became more important factors in deciding the social structure than inheritance customs. Moreover, the growth of towns during this period encouraged geographical mobility, and because the amount of capital and the skills necessary for the establishment of industry were, or could be, small, opportunities existed for social mobility. These requirements could be accumulated rapidly, so artisans with some spirit of enterprise could become merchant manufacturers more easily than in later periods. At the same time, consolidation of plots in the agricultural sector resulted in some downward mobility as those already occupying the lower rungs were pushed further down to the ranks of landless wage earners.

Consequently, Mendels argues, proto-industrialisation promoted an increase in both upward and downward status mobility. He further suggests that mobility may even have declined in the decades before the industrial revolution, which, if true, casts doubt upon the view that upward mobility was easy at this time and promoted economic progress by providing achievement incentives. In any case, it is clear that opportunities for social mobility existed and that society was open, irrespective of level of economic development.[29]

These findings notwithstanding, the timing of the change in industrial leadership and particularly the emergence of the small man, which is supposed to be characteristic of, and apparently unique to, the period of industrialisation, is difficult to explain. Fixed capital requirements, despite the prevalent economising techniques, are unlikely to have been lower at this time, given the more advanced and expensive technology, than previously. Furthermore, the difficulties created by the search for working capital, which formed the greater proportion of costs during the early period of industrialisation, were similar in both periods.

The problem of finding capital was largely a problem of finding circulating capital, for stocks of raw materials, work in progress and finished commodities, and for rents, interest and wage payments and the like; and this was a problem not unknown to merchants and employers of the "putting out" type, before the birth of the factory system. In consequence, the new industrialists took over from the older types of industry and commerce, with little change, the methods both of providing capital and of making payments. These methods were based on an elaborate and delicately balanced system of credit.[30]

It is possible that new industrial techniques and methods of organisation widened the range and even the extent of opportunities, but there is no logical reason why the openings should have been filled by men of humble origins, or even by a diverse group of individuals rather than simply by the same type as previously. Hagen, for instance, in his work on social change, proposes the notion that whatever the stage of development or social or cultural environment, entrepreneurs are drawn from a similar social background, and very rarely do they emerge from humble origins. Wide-ranging research enables him to offer the following general hypothesis: '. . . the leaders in the transition to economic growth were neither randomly distributed throughout the population nor drawn from the group that was most elite or had the greatest wealth . . . instead, they came disproportionately from some one or more less elite groups'.[31]

The view persists, nevertheless, that, particularly in the late eighteenth and early nineteenth centuries, entrepreneurs emerged from diverse social origins. The evidence for this is sparse,[32] and support for the small-man thesis is limited to a handful of exceptional and extensively documented captains of industry.[33] Systematic examination of the origins of entrepreneurship during the period of industrialisation in Britain is scarce.[34] It is important to know precisely who comprised the industrial leadership at this time, as well as those who sustained the position of entrepreneur. If the power structure did change, the implications for the interpretation of economic and social change are substantial. The purpose of this study is to provide systematic evidence from which conclusions concerning the nature of early industrial leadership can confidently be drawn.

Notes

1 H. J. Perkin, *The Origins of Modern English Society 1780–1880*, London, 1969, p. 176.

2 P. Mathias, *The First Industrial Nation*, Cambridge, 1969, pp. 157–8.

3 C. H. Lee, *A Cotton Enterprise 1795–1840. A History of M'Connel and Kennedy, fine cotton spinners*, Manchester, 1972, p. 2, refers to the flexible nature of the cotton industry at this time.

4 T. S. Ashton, *The Industrial Revolution 1760–1830*, Oxford, 1948, p. 16.

5 F. Crouzet, 'Capital formation in Great Britain during the industrial revolution', in F. Crouzet (ed.), *Capital Formation in the Industrial Revolution*, London, 1972, p. 182.

6   Lee, *M'Connel and Kennedy*, p. 2.
7   Referred to in C. Erickson, *British Industrialists: Steel and Hosiery 1850–1950*, Cambridge, 1959, p. 79.
8   Crouzet, 'Capital formation', p. 188.
9   *Ibid.*, pp. 164–5.
10   P. Mathias, preface to Crouzet (ed.), *Capital Formation*, p. viii.
11   Crouzet, 'Capital formation', p. 184.
12   Lee, *M'Connel and Kennedy*, p. 15, and Crouzet (ed.), *Capital Formation*, p. 38.
13   S. Pollard, 'Fixed capital in the industrial revolution in Britain', in Crouzet (ed.), *Capital Formation*, p. 153.
14   S. D. Chapman, 'Fixed capital formation in the British cotton industry 1770–1815', *Economic History Review*, XXIII, 1970, pp. 236–7.
15   Industry, thrift, determination.
16   Perkin, *Modern English Society*, p. 224.
17   *Ibid.*
18   J. S. Mill, *Principles*, London, 1904, p. 455.
19   Perkin, *Modern English Society*, p. 221.
20   Thrift, application, perseverance, energy, hard work, etc.
21   S. Smiles, *Self-Help*, London, 1859, p. 36.
22   *Ibid.*, p. 111.
23   E. Potter, *A Picture of a Manufacturing District*, Manchester, 1856, pp. 54–5.
24   Perkin, *Modern English Society*, p. 225.
25   S. Pollard, *The Genesis of Modern Management*, London, 1965, p. 161.
26   J. F. C. Harrison, *The Early Victorians 1832–1851*, London, 1971, p. 143.
27   Mathias, *First Industrial Nation*, pp. 157–8, and Lee, *M'Connel and Kennedy*, p. 2.
28   L. Stone, 'Social mobility in England 1500–1700', *Past and Present*, XXXIII, 1966, pp. 48–50.
29   F. F. Mendels, 'Social mobility and phases of industrialisation', *Journal of Interdisciplinary History*, VII, 1976, pp. 202–8.
30   Pollard, 'Fixed capital', in Crouzet (ed.), *Capital Formation*, p. 151.
31   E. E. Hagen, *On the Theory of Social Change*, London, 1964, p. 30.
32   S. D. Chapman, *The Early Factory Masters*, Newton Abbot, 1967, Throws some light on this subject; and Erickson, *British Industrialists*, examines the origins of entrepreneurship in the steel and hosiery

industries between 1850 and 1950.

33 Moreover, Smiles has been responsible for emphasising unduly the 'humbleness' of the origins of many of his heroes, and thus for exaggerating the role played by the small man in the early industrial leadership.

34 Whereas in the United States this is the subject of many studies.

II

Hypothesis, sources and methods

The purpose of this study is to test the commonly held belief that positions of industrial power in the eighteenth and early nineteenth centuries were open to individuals from diverse social origins, and particularly that unprecedented opportunities existed then for small men to attain the role of the entrepreneur. If opportunities were indeed great, then industries with a low capital threshold would provide a potential target for an ambitious man with little capital. In the early stages of industrialisation the initial fixed capital requirements of almost all industries were small.[1] In principle, industries at a more advanced stage of development required a higher level of entry capital and therefore provided less chance for the man with limited capital to increase his wealth and status. An exploitation of new economic opportunities, therefore, was likely to be most successful in the early, flexible stages of development of an industry. Optimum conditions for the emergence of the small man, moreover, probably existed for a short time only, and disappeared as entry requirements and the demands of working capital inevitably increased and/or profit margins fell.[2]

The social structure of investment was taken to be an appropriate indicator of the accuracy of the above hypothesis. It was thus decided to examine the origins of the successful entrepreneurs in three industries – cotton, lace and lead mining – which, in the early stage of their development, provide a suitable cross-section of size, structure and entrepreneurial type. This decision is not without methodological significance. A comparative approach to the question is used here in an attempt to control for several explanatory variables, and to reject those that, upon examination, appear unimportant. This method contains elements of counter-factual reasoning. It may be believed, for example, that fixed capital costs constituted the major obstacle to the emergence as entrepreneur of the man of limited means. If, following investigation, the social structure of investment of a particular industry exhibits no change from that known to be the case in the pre-industrial situation,[3] it may be that capital costs were too high and prevented the emergence of individuals of modest or small means.

Before this is concluded, however, a check can be made by comparison with another industry, one where capital costs are known to be minimal. If the social structure of investment again shows little or no change, the assumption can be made that fixed capital requirements alone were not inhibiting diversity in the social profile of the firm. This process, whereby the type,[4] rather than the extent, of influence can be assessed, is then reapplied to all known tangible variables, which can then be discarded or considered further as appropriate. The vital force may not be located by this procedure, but attention may be diverted from irrelevant or insignificant explanatory variables.

The first industry chosen for the purposes of this study was cotton, which emerged in an advanced stage of mechanisation at an early date, enveloped several geographical regions and is reputed to have been the classic location of self-made men.[5] Juxtaposed with this was the lace industry, which underwent technological and organisational changes later, was highly localised in the Nottingham area and had, in principle, relatively small initial capital requirements. The decision was made to consider also the lead-mining industry, whose organisational and financial structure differed significantly from the other two. During the eighteenth century it formed the primary or subsidiary means of livelihood for the majority of inhabitants in the chief mining areas, through active lead mining, smelting, selling or investing. Within the industry the scale of operation and capital investment varied greatly, from the 'penny' mines to the £80,000 soughs. This diversity of extent, which is illustrated more clearly in the lead-mining industry than in any other, suggested that the social base of investment might be very wide and would provide, certainly in terms of the potentially minimal initial capital requirements, a chance for the small man to attain a position of industrial power.

Within each industry it was necessary to select a representative group of individuals in order to examine the pattern of industrial leadership. There is no way in which a random sample of entrepreneurs at this time can be taken, because of the absence of complete sampling frames. This is not serious, however, and viable generalisations can still be made from the purposive or convenience samples that have been chosen for this study. As Charlotte Erickson said with respect to her examination of industrialists in the hosiery and steel industries, the 'samples . . . are neither "random" nor stratified, but represent the proportion of the whole population which the historical sources enable us to study. The unscientific but necessary way of selecting samples is perhaps . . . compensated for by the very high proportion of the total population which has so far been included.'[6]

For the purposes of the present study, 'samples' were chosen by the following procedures. In the cotton industry, Colquhoun's 1787 census of Arkwright-type spinning mills was used as a surrogate sampling frame. Colquhoun enumerated 145 water-powered cotton spinning factories, and the origins of the partners in each of these enterprises were investigated. It could be argued that cotton spinning on Arkwright's principle required extensive factory premises from the start,[7] and for this reason it was considered apposite to determine the extent to which another 'gate of entry' into entrepreneurship in the cotton industry was utilised by ambitious men of limited capital. Cotton spinning by Crompton's mule technique could be carried out in smaller units and was in many ways a more feasible method by which an individual of this type could succeed. Moreover, production by this technique was partly organised in small units until the mid-nineteenth century,[8] so fixed capital requirements, at least, were surmountable, and opportunities for the small man persisted in the long term.

For the purpose of this study the earliest known census of Crompton's mule, undertaken in 1811, was used. Well over 300 firms were listed, with a total of more than a thousand partners, and because the enumeration divided the firms into areas the choice of entrepreneurs to be studied was narrowed on the basis of an area sample. Oldham and Bolton, in many ways contrasting districts, particularly with respect to type of product and scale of operation, were thus selected, with the aim of locating and examining all the entrepreneurs there.

The lace industry, which transferred to powered technology in the second decade of the nineteenth century, offered, in principle, and particularly in its boom period, a means by which an individual could increase his capital quickly. The prospects for this, however, were short-lived, and a large proportion of the many men who entered the industry in the early 1820s, when machine prices were temporarily low and wages temporarily high, failed in the 1826 slump and in the years following.

Because of the small scale and short-term nature of many of the enterprises at this time, it was considered appropriate to examine the more durable entrepreneurs who were still functioning in the late 1820s.[9] In 1829 a petition in favour of a restriction of hours[10] was signed by all owners of one or more lace machines, and this constituted a sampling frame. It was decided to investigate the origins of 700 signatories. The remainder[11] were excluded on the grounds that they were operating in parts of England distant from Nottingham, and would not only be difficult to trace but the return would be inadequate with respect to time and effort expended.

No discrete period of peak activity or exceptional opportunity existed in the lead-mining industry. Nevertheless, because technological developments within the industry accelerated after 1700, and because activity declined after 1800, the individuals selected for examination in this study were those operating during the eighteenth century. It is clearly impossible to select a systematic and representative sample, as thousands of petty and transient investors were attracted, together with those with more considerable and long-term interests. Nevertheless, it was hoped that the sample arrived at would include representatives from each type.

This study centres on the sough masters, the organisers of, and investors in lead mine drainage schemes, who were both substantial capitalists and themselves investors in the mines. At least 200 sough partnerships existed in the Derbyshire lead-mining field, involving over a thousand investors, so a representative sample of 25% of the soughs was chosen,[12] and an attempt made to trace the 400 associated individuals. By excluding the small scale mines, the sample is skewed towards the larger investors. This is justifiable on the grounds that although very little capital investment was necessary to become a small lead miner, and this activity was thus open to almost anyone, it was very unusual for much profit to be made by the small man and rarely was long-term success achieved. Moreover, the investment even of the larger capitalists was frequently smaller[13] than that of entrepreneurs in other industries. The sample employed, therefore, although skewed, is purposive.

As the main interest of this work is the social structure of investment during the early period of industrialisation, a means of categorising this is required. Occupation has been used in this study as an indicator of social status, but the problem exists of classifying occupations in a historical perspective. Clearly there are difficulties in applying a fixed (static) classification to changing (dynamic) historical conditions. In order to provide a quantitative assessment of the social structure of investment, and to judge roughly the extent of social mobility in an individual's rise to entrepreneurship, an occupational classification was devised.[14] This was no easy task. The nature and limitations of information yielded by the sources had to be taken into account, and classes adopted which would be applicable, if with some reservation, to the period of over a hundred years covered by this study. Further complications emerged from the fact that both rural and urban areas were covered, that occupations varied among industries, and that the rank order for any one industry might change over time. Allowance was made for these potential weaknesses within this study and is referred to where appropriate.

Unfortunately, none of the valuable twentieth-century occupational classifications[15] was directly applicable to the study, since occupational conditions have changed and so have the perceptions of occupational differences. A suitable alternative exists, however, and Charlotte Erickson's classification has been adapted.[16]

As a result, the occupations that emerge are divided into four broad socio-economic groups with the recognition that limited opportunities exist for refinement. A more precise or detailed rank order would have hindered, or broken down under, long-term comparisons.

The classification was constructed as follows: Class I included all members of the aristocracy and gentry, large businessmen, professional people such as doctors, lawyers, clergy, and large farmers and landowners. Skilled craftsmen working on their own account, retail traders and yeomen comprised social class II. Class III contained skilled craftsmen working for another, and very small landholders[17] such as husbandmen. Semi-skilled or unskilled workers and agricultural labourers were placed in class IV.[18] In each case the occupation referred to is that held by the individual either prior to, or, in the lead-mining industry, simultaneously with his position as an entrepreneur.

Throughout the text, references are made to 'small' or 'modest' men with respect to origin. In terms of the classification just described, 'modest' men are those whose occupation lay within class II, while 'small' men have occupational backgrounds in class III or IV.

The categories, however, were not rigidly enforced; that is, the 'names' of occupations were not regarded as binding. Where supplementary evidence revealed the inadequacy or inaptness of the category of a particular individual, an adjustment was made. That is, in each case the individual was placed in the category appropriate to the evidence. Although the occupation of each individual in the study was derived from a variety of sources, it was typically based on self-description, and as a result the accuracy of the classification must be questioned. Although individuals are more likely to be honest about their occupation than, say, the extent of their wealth, elements of ambiguity inevitably occur. It is possible that self-description leads to rank or status inflation, and the chance of this increases when there is no internal or external check upon the individual's self-designation. A further limitation stems from the vagueness of some conventional descriptions, which raises categorisation problems. Some conventions, moreover, change over time or differ from place to place and from class to class. In the light of these potential weaknesses historical evidence and insight must be utilised in interpreting the available self-description.

There are several terms specific to this study that are either ambiguous or in some other way exaccerbate the problem of placing individuals in a social occupational structure. The description 'miner', for instance, can cause confusion. During the eighteenth century the expression usually applied to a manual worker, but in at least one instance in this study it referred to an individual, clearly of some wealth, who owned shares in many lead mines. In practice, however, information on individual cases was generally acquired which distinguished the various types. The status of an individual as an employer or employee is often obscure. The unqualified title 'shoemaker' or 'machine maker' does not distinguish ownership of the means of production or otherwise. Additional information is necessary, and this, fortunately, is frequently available, but if a substantiated answer does not subsequently emerge, then it is necessary to resort, with reservations and qualifications, to informed guesswork.

Classification difficulties also arise from the term 'yeoman'. Typically this was used to denote a landowning farmer, so the problem becomes one of assessing the scale of ownership. At various times the owner of a small plot of land, a large landowning farmer, or individuals occupying intermediate stages have similarly been described as 'yeoman'. During the eighteenth century the yeoman was an individual who owned a substantial piece of land, frequently kept animals, and was well established financially. In Laslett's view, '. . . a yeoman had to be a fairly substantial owner (not renter) of land which he had to work himself; for he emphatically did not come under the idleness rule which defined gentlemanliness'.[19] Both large and small landowners, however, could be equally described as 'farmer', 'yeoman' or 'husbandman', though the latter was usually small-scale and frequently involved in an additional occupation, such as lead mining. Both the term 'yeoman', which was usually placed in class II, and the occupational description 'smelter', which could, apparently, refer to either employer or employee, required further information in order to ascertain the appropriate classification.

It may be argued that the classification proposed is weighted towards the lower end of the occupational categories. This, however, has methodological significance, and can be justified on the grounds that it provides a clearer, though perhaps exaggerated, indication of the role of men of small means in the industrial leadership of eighteenth and early nineteenth-century Britain that forms one aspect of the hypothesis. That is, in illustrating the social structure of investment, an index that is constructed with a downward bias, and then reveals little activity from small men, strengthens a conclusion that a substantial change in business leadership had not occurred. If, however, the role of the small man appears from the investigation to be significant, further evidence would be required to test whether the result was affected by index bias. This approximates to Fogel's optimisation technique,[20] or to the mathematician's concept of upper and lower bound.

Although this study is to some extent concerned with social mobility, implicitly at least, it is not possible to measure distances or extent, nor to follow through an individual's experience of social mobility. Moreover, not all entrepreneurs at this, or any other, time are of equivalent status; though in this study, for the purpose of simplification, they are all considered to be class I. Although mobility is of interest, the emphasis is on constructing a social profile of firms through an analysis of the social background of each entrepreneur.

The most intractable problem in a study of this nature is insufficient or inappropriate data. When 'systematic' error is likely to be great, classical statistical tests are not applicable. Within the context of this study, the tests of historical statistics must consequently be tests of consistency, compatibility and common sense, using all available relevant knowledge. The more fragmentary the evidence, the more important the role of outside knowledge. When attempting to make generalisations from incomplete data, as here, it is necessary to make the limitations explicit and to specify the use of any estimation procedures as clearly and fully as possible, so that they can be adequately checked and criticised.[21]

Evidence to test the hypothesis was sought from a variety of sources. Having selected the individuals to be examined, information concerning their backgrounds was obtained from local records. Several collections of family papers and probate inventories provided valuable insight into the origins and experience of the Derbyshire sough masters. This evidence was supplemented by printed local primary sources, such as parish registers, newspapers and directories. Theses and secondary literature provided incidental information. The origins of the early cotton spinners were discovered by reference to a variety of Lancashire manuscript collections, business records, local rate and valuation books, and directories. Remaining gaps were filled by consulting newspapers and an extensive secondary literature. Information from apprenticeship registers, partnership deeds, rate books, local directories and poll books was combined to form a picture of the origins of the 1829 lace manufacturers, and the 1851 census was consulted to indicate their subsequent fortunes.

Throughout the course of the research it has been necessary to make certain assumptions and estimations which have not always enjoyed the backing of concrete data, but without this procedure it would have been impossible to continue. This was particularly the case when allocating occupational titles to the crude social groupings described above. Some of the categorisations are open to criticism but, because of the nature of the information, no alternative approach was apparent.

Notes

1   At least, the requirements were less than they were to become, but not necessarily than they had been. Moreover, industries at this stage were flexible in structure and receptive to change.

2   Which in many industries occurred after 1815. Lee, *M'Connel and Kennedy*, pp. 139–41, refers to high profits before 1815, and P. L. Cottrell, *Industrial Finance 1830–1914*, London, 1980, p. 24, indicates falling profit levels in the second quarter of the nineteenth century.

3   Typically, as far as is known, industrial investors in the early modern period were wealthy or moderately wealthy individuals despite potential opportunities for the man of limited means.

4   That is, positive, negative or neutral.

5 That is, it was a new industry, exhibiting flexibility and requiring a low level of initial capital investment. It is these features in particular that are believed to have facilitated the emergence of the small man.

6 Erickson, *British Industrialists*, p. 7.

7 And could therefore be very expensive.

8 R. Lloyd Jones and A. A. Le Roux, 'The size of firms in the cotton industry: Manchester 1815–1841', *Economic History Review*, XXXIII, 1980, p. 73.

9 Only a small proportion of those in business in the mid-1820s.

10 Worked by lace machines.

11 Some 300.

12 Designed to include examples of each type of sough.

13 The majority of investments lay in the region of £20–£40, though investments approaching £1,000 were not uncommon.

14 While being aware of the many factors involved in social status, social class and social mobility, it is necessary, in a large-scale study of this nature, to select a unit of measurement that can be determined by systematic means. Occupation is one such indicator of social status; it is a more or less objective and relatively easily obtainable datum, and while it does not contain all aspects of status, information relating to the other factors, such as manners, income and authority positions, cannot be obtained with any degree of consistency in the period under consideration.

15 For example, those of Glass, Moser and Hall, the Population Investigation Committee, the Registrar General and the Social Survey.

16 Erickson, *British Industrialists*, p. 11.

17 The term refers to tenant rather than owner.

18 This classification also corresponds to that used by K. Wrightson and D. Levine, *Poverty and Piety in an English Village: Terling 1525–1700*, London, 1979, p. 34.

19 Peter Laslett, *The World we have lost*, London, 1965, p. 43.

20 Which he used in his examination of US railways, R. W. Fogel, *Railroads and American Economic Growth: Essays in Econometric History*, Baltimore, 1964, p. 20, pp. 21–8.

21 R. Floud, *An Introduction to Quantitative Methods for Historians*, London, 1973, p. 175.

III

Lead mining in Derbyshire: organisation and finance

A variety of systems of mine finance and organisation were developed and employed during the long history of the lead-mining industry. Throughout the eighteenth century a 'cope' system prevailed, where a small gang of miners, any number between two and twelve, examined a mineral vein, judged the quality and quantity of the ore exposed, and assessed the difficulty of extracting it. On the basis of their examination, the miners formalised an agreement with the agent or the owner of the mine on the sum to be paid for each load of ore. This cope bargain was struck for a specified length of time, known as a reckoning, which was usually between six and thirteen weeks, and was renewable. The agreed amount was calculated as a proportion of the anticipated value of the ore, thus the system was a gamble for the owner as well as for the copers.[1] In practice gains fluctuated, but copers generally earned considerably more than miners on wage work, or than the local agricultural labourer.[2]

The miner himself held shares in the majority of modest excavations. Evidence indicates that during the eighteenth century countless small mines existed which were owned and worked independently by groups of labouring miners. Once a particular mine was cleared out, or if it was found to contain insufficient accessible ore, the group moved elsewhere in the hope of greater profits.[3] Lead mining was a notably speculative industry; it was impossible to predict the financial return of any individual vein of ore. James Pilkington, a contemporary local commentator, assessed the situation thus: 'It must be confessed that there is scarcely any business which has so much of the appearance of adventure . . . but . . . entire blanks are seldom drawn. Some quantity of ore is generally met with, though in undertakings of this kind the profits are not always adequate to the expence [*sic*] of pursuing them.'[4]

Despite the obvious limitations, prospecting in the Derbyshire field was encouraged by means of the codification of 'laws and customs'. This code, first laid down in 1288, clearly favoured the miner, as it permitted, in principle, a search for lead ore on any piece of land within the Derbyshire mining area, except churchyards or orchards. A miner who found ore, or who suspected a vein of containing ore, was required by the laws to inform the Barmaster of the Liberty[5] of his intention to excavate, and to produce what was known as a 'freeing dish' of lead ore from the vein. In return the miner was granted two 'founder meers'[6] in which to work, and a right of access to his mine from the nearest highway. A labouring miner, however, rarely had access to sufficient capital to work independently a mine thus obtained. As a result, shares in the mine were distributed in twenty-fourth parts, or in fractions or multiples of this,[7] and each shareholder became responsible for the cost of excavating, and associated expenses, in proportion to the size of his holding. If a partner died or withdrew during the life of the mine, his shares were divided among the remaining partners, or sold externally, often in small parts of shares.[8] This partnership system tended to attract funds from small investors, whose initial capital commitment might be as little as £1. It also facilitated the practice, common among the wealthier investors, of spreading interests over a large number of mines. By this means the risks involved in mining speculation were minimised.

As the scale and extent of mining operations grew during the seventeenth century a new set of regulations were formulated, and the rate of duty – that is, the proportion of the output donated to the proprietor in either dressed ore or smelted lead – became more flexible and reflected more appropriately the state of the industry. The rates varied according to conditions within the industry and were generally at their highest during periods of rapid growth.[9] In general, however, the law continued to favour the emergence of the small man and reinforced the authorisation of any individual to dig and search for

veins of ore without being liable or accountable to the owners or
occupiers of the soil for any consequent damage to the surface of the
land, or even to growing crops.[10] Men of limited means were also
given opportunities to participate in the industry through the
potentially small size of shares and the ease with which they were sold
and transferred.[11] The major impediment to the long-term success of
the small man was the payment of duty to the proprietors.[12] This was
an onerous tax which many small investors found insuperable, though
in practice the tithe owners did not exact it so rigorously from the
small miners as they did from the richer speculators, who frequently
had alternative sources of income to ease the pressures of working
capital requirements.

Until the seventeenth century, while the industry was labour-
intensive, initiative in lead mining generally came from the working
miners who employed simple, inexpensive techniques, and frequently
combined mining activities with the working of a farm or
smallholding. The miner worked a shallow mine until all accessible
ore was extracted, or until water in the workings made it impossible
to continue without expensive drainage schemes, whereupon he began
excavations elsewhere.[13] This tradition persisted, and during the
eighteenth century many small owner-occupied mines continued to be
operated alongside larger ventures. Each was worked by small
partnerships, or possibly by single men, and the enterprise might be
full-time or part-time, determined by the quality of deposits and the
price of lead. During the eighteenth century, however, as the degree
of proficiency and the level of capital investment increased, a gradual
but consistent movement took place away from a system whereby
miners shared directly with owners in the risks and profits of the
enterprise, towards a capitalistic employer/employee relationship. As
a result, the miner lost not only his independence but also the
opportunity to make high profits. He received instead a regular wage,
which in practice was frequently more advantageous financially.[14]

By the end of the eighteenth century lead mining was no longer an
activity appropriate for the small man; it had become capital-intensive
and thus open only to those with substantial assets. Expenses required
for installing pumping engines for drainage and deepening shafts

increased in size and urgency at this time, as the richer shallow ore bodies were exhausted. The lead merchants, who provided much of the necessary capital for these activities, purchased 'duty ore' from the royalty owners and took the output of the small mines, or the share due to the partner, in return for cash. This eliminated the necessity for the miners to accumulate stocks and wait for the market, which would have created working capital pressures. It was common, during the second half of the eighteenth century, for the several processes associated with lead mining to be integrated by a single individual, in practice a member of one of the wealthy local families, whose investments were diversified. His duties included the organisation of mines, soughs, smelt mills, together with the marketing.[15]

During the eighteenth century much of the capital for the lead-mining industry was provided by the landowner, in other words the mineral proprietor,[16] as well as by the lead merchant.[17] The immediate concern of the proprietors was to ascertain that their mines were regularly and effectively worked in order to maximise output, and cover costs. When large-scale and expensive development work was required, however, particularly the long drainage levels driven in the late eighteenth and early nineteenth century, the proprietors tended to finance and work the mines direct.[18]

Lead mining in the second half of the eighteenth century was characterised by the sough. Soughs were drainage levels designed to remove water from mines and thus permit more lead to be extracted. A peculiar feature of the Derbyshire field was the frequency of mines worked by companies or partnerships insufficiently large to execute any major works, but adequate to maintain a steady development above sough level. A type of company unique to the county was one which owned shares in, and drove a sough, on behalf of the mining groups, in return for a proportion of the ore which the sough had rendered accessible. Investment in an enterprise such as this was clearly a gamble, as it was impossible to predict the quantity and value of ore, if any, that would be unearthed. Moreover, overlapping or duplicated enterprises, undertaken by competing organisations, frequently reduced the gains to be made. This was the result of the absence of systematic planning of a large area, caused by the complexity of small mine and sough companies.[19]

The entrenched position of the small mining concerns in the High Peak district prevented the monopoly of large, vertically integrated companies which engaged in mining, soughing and smelting. Increasingly the workers in the smaller concerns were wage-earners employed by non-labouring investors, but generally enterprises remained small in size and large in number. This feature continued into the nineteenth century, and as late as 1872, for instance, nearly 200 mining concerns existed in Derbyshire, 138 of which produced less than five tons of ore each during that year.[20] This suggests that opportunities for the small man remained and that lead mining had become very much a subsidiary occupation for those involved.

During the eighteenth century capital was not invested in large concerns except in two distinct fields of activity, the driving of drainage soughs and lead smelting, though even in these areas small enterprises persisted. Many of the drainage soughs were driven by partnerships formed specifically for the purpose, which reserved a share, a sixteenth or a quarter of the ore mined from the area drained by the sough. The terms of the agreement between the miners and the soughers usually included provision for the latter to maintain and repair the sough. If, despite this, the sough were neglected the miner might carry out repairs while making appropriate adjustments in the payments due. A reciprocal arrangement usually held that if the miners were negligent in their duties, thereby effectively reducing the income of the soughers, then the soughers were empowered to take over the working of the mine.[21]

The lead-mining and sough partnerships varied considerably in terms of social structure, resources and endurance. They ranged from associations of a small number of partners each investing several thousands of pounds to groups of shareholders where each individual contributed as little as £20.[22] These latter were the small men whose development and progress are crucial to the central hypothesis of this study and who are, therefore, of particular interest.[23] Some partnerships existed for a year or two only, others operated successfully for more than fifty years. The system of share splitting not only gave investment opportunities to individuals with limited resources, but also permitted wealthier investors to spread their risks over a wide range of mines and soughs.[24] Lead mining and sough partnerships faced considerable problems during the first few years of the nineteenth century, when ore shoots became exhausted and deeper workings suffered from influxes of water which caused a sharp fall in mining output and at the same time raised its cost. Many smaller investors were displaced also by the technological developments of the late eighteenth century. The new machinery required heavy capital investment. Thus the environment within which the 'small' man could operate ceased to exist when the easier seams were worked out. That is, with greater difficulties in mining, there was a tendency towards more capital-intensive production methods.

For the purposes of this study the lead mining entrepreneurs selected for examination were those who invested in the mine soughs rather than in the mines themselves. Several factors influenced this decision. The mines in Derbyshire numbered many thousands, though a precise enumeration does not exist. The enormous variation in the size, value and longevity of the mines, together with the absence of a complete sampling frame, impeded the search for a representative sample. A representative group of soughs, however, was more easily obtained. The majority of mining enterprises, moreover, were minute, unprofitable and short-lived. Most individuals would be in a position to invest in a mine of this nature, but the chance of achieving any upward social mobility by this means was remote. The initial capital investment in soughs varied, and although it was generally greater than that required for the small mine, the cost of sough shares could be low.[25] As a result, opportunities did exist for the individual with a small quantity of capital to invest in a sough, and if this enterprise were successful further investment was possible, together with sustained upward mobility.

It is appropriate to consider the extent of the available opportunities for a wage-earning lead miner to become an investor in an eighteenth-century sough enterprise. Lead mining was not well paid by comparison with other occupations requiring a comparable skill;[26] wages, moreover, were subject to considerable fluctuation.[27] Many lead miners, however, supplemented their income by other means, most commonly by working a smallholding, which was apparently considered to be prestigious. J. W. Gough has shown that those labourers who devoted almost their entire lives to mining frequently described themselves proudly as husbandmen or yeomen.[28] It is clear that those miners who joined together in partnerships, each contributing a small amount of capital and sharing the gains, were in a position to benefit, or to lose, much more than the working miner employed by a larger company. It was risky, however, for an individual of limited capital to enter into a partnership of this nature. The lead-mining industry was peculiarly speculative, and the absence of sound financial backing might quickly result in bankruptcy. In spite of the obvious hazards, the limited opportunities for the wage-earning lead miner lent great appeal to the prospect of operating independently.

Evidence suggests that, initially, very little capital investment in the Derbyshire lead mines was recruited from within the industry itself. Before 1700 only small amounts of capital were required for the majority of ventures, most of which was provided by local landowners. From the early eighteenth century, however, capital trickled into the industry from a variety of sources, and was invested in larger quantities after 1750. Nevertheless the scale of enterprise continued to exhibit substantial diversity; and the great variations in the resources of the mining companies, and in the size of shares held within each company, eased the attraction of capital from a wide social base. 'A list of investors in lead mines,' Burt comments, 'reads like a local trades' directory until well into the second half of the eighteenth century',[29] but it is frequently assumed that two groups of individuals only predominated in providing the necessary investment; the lead smelters and merchants, and the owners of the land which contained the mineral resources.

The Derbyshire lead merchants tended to diversify their interests, particularly into the coal and iron industries of south Yorkshire. Similarly the Yorkshire coal and iron masters extended their investment activities into the Derbyshire lead-mining field. The mines of Eyam Edge, for example, were extensively developed in the eighteenth century by a group of men which included six lead merchants, four iron masters and several landowners whose fortunes had been made in lead, coal and iron ventures.[30] The large profits made in several of the mining and smelting concerns led a number of successful merchant investors to transfer their newly acquired or enlarged wealth to the greater security and prestige of land ownership. The acquisition of land was still at this stage a clear indication of upward status mobility, as it had been for centuries previously.

Several families, however, retained a longer-term commitment to the industry; the Barker family[31] and the Wilkinson family[32] are notable examples. Early in the eighteenth century William Barker, steward to the Duke of Devonshire,[33] invested in several mines and owned a smelting mill. William's sons, Alexander, George and John, carried on the business after his death, and by 1750 the family owned four smelting mills and shared a fifth with the Milnes[34] and the Wilkinsons, lead merchants who bought most of the Barkers' pig lead. In 1759 the Barker brothers formed a partnership with John and Richard Wilkinson, and the relationship continued with Richard's sons John and Isaac.[35] Because of the fluidity of personnel within the industry, however, few further instances exist of such enduring intergenerational interest.

Local manuscripts[36] provide clear illustration of the heavy involvement in lead mining of landowners and Derbyshire gentry.[37] The less extensive participation of yeomen farmers and small businessmen in the seventeenth and early eighteenth centuries is also indicated.[38] After 1750 the pattern changed, and the contribution of the lead smelters to the capital formation of the industry became much more prominent.[39]

Towards the end of the century several of the large investors in lead channelled capital into the infant local cotton industry. The Evans family, for instance, owned shares in a diverse collection of mines and in the mid-eighteenth century purchased smelting and rolling mills at Derby.[40] In 1783 George Evans independently founded a cotton mill community in Darley Abbey,[41] and shortly afterwards established a bank in Derby. This bank, Crompton, Evans & Co., provided working capital for both Richard Arkwright and

Samuel Oldknow in their textile operations.[42] The Spencer family, extensive mine shareholders in the Wirksworth area,[43] also subsequently diversified into the cotton trade. Samuel Simpson became a cotton merchant and manufacturer in Manchester, and his sister Mary married Richard Arkwright junior.[44] In 1787 Samuel and his brother John joined Thomas Whittenbury and Richard Arkwright junior in a Manchester cotton spinning enterprise.[45]

These examples also provide some illustration of the extent of the interrelationships among members of the Derbyshire gentry during the eighteenth century. Connections and bonds were formed both socially and through business activities. Intermarriage was common and purposefully structured: as a result, a desirable expansion in the family circle took place which increased the potential supply of talent and capital available for business enterprises. Moreover the phenomenon ensured the stability of the firm as well as the continuity of personnel within it.

Early in the nineteenth century, when the fortunes of lead mining in Derbyshire deteriorated, the price of ore fell dramatically and mine drainage became an increasingly expensive and intractable problem. As a result the structure of investment changed. Previously organised by large investors or smelters, many mines came to be operated instead by small partnerships of minor local businessmen or tradesmen. Shoemakers, builders, grocers, rope manufacturers and woolcombers,[46] who formed the majority, combined their primary occupation with mining, which for many, given the state of the industry, was an unfortunate decision. The transfer of capital into textile production, which began late in the eighteenth century by those individuals previously heavily committed to lead, continued with growing momentum in the early nineteenth.[47] The removal of the interest of these major local investors ensured the irreversible demise of the industry in Derbyshire.

Most of the capital for the lead-mining industry, throughout its long history, was recruited locally.[48] There were two significant exceptions. In 1720 the London Lead Company, a Quaker group who pursued extensive mining interests in Wales and Northumberland, sought to diversify the geographical location of their activities. As a result of connections with several local families, the company turned its attention to the Derbyshire mines.[49] It assumed control of several large enterprises and established a group of smelting units. Success was only temporary; by 1775 large losses had been sustained, and all its Derbyshire leases were surrendered by 1792.[50] The second exception was the London New Lead Company, whose influence upon the Derbyshire industry from the late eighteenth century and well into the nineteenth was substantial.[51] The majority of shareholders in both companies were from London, mostly small businessmen who sought additional cash to finance their social aspirations.[52]

Since our attention centres on the investors in soughs, it is appropriate to identify the two types of sough and the corresponding sough masters. The first type was small, driven to drain a specific mine only. In this case the sough and the equivalent mine partnership lists were usually identical. The larger soughs were planned to free a group of mines of water, and the associated proprietors were substantial capitalists who frequently held shares in additional mines and soughs, and invested also in unrelated activities such as cotton spinning or banking.[53]

It is possible that the sough of the former type presented, in the early eighteenth century, an opportunity to the man with limited capital resources to become an investor in and potentially a beneficiary of an expanding industry. Many investors became partners in soughs because of a financial interest in the mines which the sough was designed to drain.[54] The expense of many soughs was substantial and usually shared among a large group of partners.[55] As a result the quantity of capital contributed initially by each individual, though variable, could be small, and was in any case by no means as great as that required for the establishment of a cotton mill, or for other contemporary industrial ventures.[56] Nevertheless, investment was risky, return was unpredictable, and, as a precaution, the interest of many individuals was diversified among a number of mines and soughs.

The smallest capitalists did not become involved in the drainage of their mines; responsibility for this was assumed by the wealthier

individuals to whom 'composition' was paid. The larger mining
capitalists typically shared the cost of draining their own mines. A
variety of financial arrangements were formulated between soughers
and mine owners. In some cases the soughers agreed to drive the
drainage level to the mines at their own expense, until a mine was
relieved of water and became workable once more. The miners then
paid 'composition' or 'cope'[57] to the sough masters. Alternatively, if a
sough was driven along a rake vein[58] the soughers took meers[59] in
this, and considerable financial gains were commonly made from the
ore then mined.[60]

As mines varied greatly in size, cost, value and profit levels, so too
did the soughs. Cromford Sough, for instance, extended for two
miles, and its cost was reckoned to have been in the region of
£30,000,[61] though it seems that Meerbrook Sough, three miles in
length, was the most expensive to drive. Work began in 1772 and
was finally completed in 1848 at a cost of £80,000.[62] Evidence
suggests, however, that the typical sum expended in sough
construction was in the region of £500,[63] and the return on this
investment was likely to be several times larger. It was in this type of
sough particularly that opportunities existed for the man of small
means to achieve upward social mobility. The following chapter, by
considering the social structure of investment in soughs, examines the
extent to which those opportunities were taken.

Notes

1   Nellie Kirkham, *Derbyshire Lead Mining*, Truro, 1968, p. 22.
2   *Ibid.*, p. 23.
3   *Ibid.*, p. 24.
4   James Pilkington, *A View of the Present State of Derbyshire*, 1978, vol.
    I, p. 129.
5   A local official (administrator).
6   Twenty-nine yards.
7   Shares of 1/168 and 1/192 were commonplace, and shares as small as
    1/2,304 were recorded, though rarely. More evidence is presented in
    Appendix I and R. Gould, 'A Study of the Capital Formation and
    Working Conditions in the Wirksworth Lead Mines, 1700–1900',

unpublished B.A. dissertation, University of Nottingham, 1975, p. 7.

8 Gould, *op. cit.*, p. 8.
9 Particularly 1780–1815.
10 John Farey, *General View of the Agriculture and Minerals of Derbyshire*, London, 1811, vol. 1, p. 357.
11 *Ibid.*, p. 370.
12 *Ibid.*, p. 333.
13 Arthur Raistrick and Bernard Jennings, *Lead Mining in the Pennines*, London, 1965, p. 182.
14 R. Burt, 'The Lead Industry of England and Wales 1700–1880', unpublished Ph.D. Thesis, University of London, 1971, p. 269.
15 Raistrick and Jennings, *Lead Mining*, p. 180.
16 *Ibid.*, p. 183.
17 Often the same person.
18 Raistrick and Jennings, *Lead Mining*, pp. 191–4.
19 *Ibid.*, p. 224.
20 *Victoria County History of Derby*, vol. II, p. 332.
21 Raistrick and Jennings, *Lead Mining*, p. 249.
22 In practice an investment of £1 or even less was possible.
23 Although it was possible that a small shareholder in one mine or sough could be a large shareholder in another, the evidence available shows that, on the whole, small shareholders in one were also small shareholders in others and large shareholders were consistently so. See Appendix I.
24 Evidence of which is presented in Chapter IV.
25 Usually approximately £20.
26 Local agricultural labourers earned less, though urban artisans probably fared better, certainly towards the end of the period.
27 Raistrick and Jennings, *Lead Mining*, p. 297.
28 J. W. Gough, *The Mines of Mendip*, Oxford, 1930, p. 126.
29 Burt, 'Lead Industry', p. 106.
30 The ironmasters were all business associates of William Spencer of Cannon Hall, near Barnsley, son-in-law of Benjamin Ashton, a Derbyshire lead miner/gentleman.
31 Barker Collection D812 1735/6; D808/809 1743/4, D.R.O.; T. N. Ince, *Pedigrees of Families in and about Wirksworth*, 1860, p. 133; G. G. Hopkinson, 'Five generations of lead mining', *Derbyshire Archaeological Journal*, LXXVIII, 1958, pp. 10–11.
32 Woolley mss 6679/219–222, D.R.O.; Bagshaw Collection 8/4/2177, J.R.L.; Deeds 846 (1713) 23 (1764) 37 (1779), D.P.L.

33   A position of some status.

34   Devonshire Papers 132/1–133/1, Chatsworth House; Ince, *Pedigrees*, p. 359. Nellie Kirkham, 'Okenedge, Streaks, and Watergrove soughs', *Bulletin of the Peak District Mines Historical Society*, III, 1967, p. 200.

35   Raistrick and Jennings, *Lead Mining*, p. 256.

36   Especially the Gell and Wolley mss.

37   For instance the Gells and the Hurts.

38   Listed in Gould, 'Wirksworth Lead Mines', p. 16; and my thesis, p. 51.

39   *Hurts:* Bailey 1781 Directory; L. Willies, 'Cupola lead smelting in Derbyshire 1737–1900', *Bulletin of the Peak District Mines Historical Society*, IV, 1969, p. 108. *Nightingales:* Woolley mss 6680, f. 95, D.R.O.; and Devonshire Papers 132/1, Chatsworth House. *Barker and Wilkinson:* Barker Collection D808/9, 812, D.R.O.; Woolley mss 6679/219–222, D.R.O.

40   Woolley mss 6684/218 (1769); Woolley mss 6667, f. 82, D.R.O.

41   D. Peters, *Darley Abbey: from Monastery to Industrial Community*, Buxton, 1974, pp. 25 and 30.

42   R. S. Fitton and A. P. Wadsworth, *The Strutts and the Arkwrights 1758–1830*, Manchester, 1958, pp. 80 and 104.

43   Gould, 'Wirksworth Lead Mines', p. 22.

44   Chapman, *Factory Masters*, p. 95.

45   Elizabeth Raffald, *The Manchester Directory for the Year 1772*; 'Schedule of deeds relating to property in Miller Street factory yard concerning Richard Arkwright and the Simpsons, 1786', M/c 1120–1159, ms in M.C.L.

46   Chapter IV provides further information on this.

47   The Hurts, Gells and Nightingales provide examples of this phenomenon.

48   From those groups already outlined earlier in the chapter.

49   Raistrick and Jennings, *Lead Mining*, p. 123.

50   Gould, 'Wirksworth Lead Mines', p. 32.

51   Known primarily for its activities at the Goodluck mine in Wirksworth.

52   Gould, 'Wirksworth Lead Mines', p. 39.

53   See Chapter IV for elucidation.

54   The soughs within the Eyam Great Vein complex provide examples in this category.

55   Cromford sough, for instance, initially recruited 150 partners.

56 £200 was sufficient to set up as a modest brewer: P. Mathias, *The Brewing Industry in England 1700–1830*, Cambridge, 1959. Several hundred pounds was required for buildings and equipment in the early cotton industry.

57 Typically one-sixth of all ore got below that level, though it might be as much as a third. T. D. Ford and J. H. Rieuwerts, *Lead Mining in the Peak District*, Bakewell, 1968, p. 23.

58 A rake vein is a major vein running across country for a mile or more, consisting of minerals filling a fracture or fissure in the limestone which is usually nearly vertical.

59 A unit of measurement – thirty-two yards in length and whatever width or depth the vein happened to be.

60 If, however, as was sometimes the case, these veins were owned already by the miners, it was agreed that the soughers should pay for any ore that they thus obtained.

61 S. Glover, *The Peak Guide*, Derby, 1830, p. 66.

62 F. White (ed.), *History Gazetteer and directory of the county of Derby*, Sheffield, 1857.

63 Nellie Kirkham, 'Eyam Edge mines and soughs, part 4', *Bulletin of the Peak District Mines Historical Society*, III, 1966, p. 107.

IV

The sough masters

This chapter examines the social structure of investment in the Derbyshire soughs. Of particular concern is the type and degree of relationship, if any, between the size of a sough and its social profile. For example, individuals with associated interests in lead, or members of the local gentry, might be expected to comprise the principal investors in the larger enterprises, whereas the smaller soughs, requiring less capital outlay, were more likely to attract funds from a socially diverse group of people. The hypothesis that the smaller enterprise provided a means by which the individual with little capital might achieve a position of industrial leadership through upward mobility is tested.

A selection of sough masters in each district[1] was investigated with particular reference to social background, occupational interest and career pattern, and were classified according to the criteria indicated in Chapter II. The results of the survey, based on a representative 25 per cent sample[2] of the Derbyshire soughs are presented in the following tables according to area. The composite table (4.1) clearly indicates the predominance of high-status occupational backgrounds based on land and lead pursuits. Retail, textile and professional activities and manual occupations together comprise the interest of 14 per cent of the sample of sough masters. The survey suggests that the man of humble origin played only a small part in the sough-driving activities of the Derbyshire lead-mining field.

In the Wirksworth/Cromford area (Table 4.2) the eighteenth-century soughs were financed and organised principally by individuals whose primary interest was farming, and less extensively by those occupied in one of the various processes within the lead-mining industry; lead miners and other skilled manual workers (class III) formed a significant proportion (19 per cent) of the sough masters in this area. It was particularly in the Wirksworth/Cromford region that the long, expensive soughs were driven, in which the contribution of an individual partner might exceed a thousand pounds. For this reason, most investors there were interested in a single sough only, unlike other areas where a diversity of investment was common.

Table 4.1   *Known occupations of the entire sample of sough proprietors*

Occupation/rank	Social class	No. of men	% of known total
1. Land			
Gentry	I	104	28·0
Yeoman	II	28	6·4
Esquire	I	23	7·6
Farmer	I/II[b]	17	4·5
Landowner	I	11	3·0
Husbandman	III	3	0·8
2. Lead			
Smelter	I	45	12·2
Lead merchant	I	28	7·6
Miner	III	27	7·5
Mineral agent	I	9	2·6
Mine owner	I	7	1·9
Barmaster	I	3	0·8
Steward	I	2	0·5
Mine overseer	I	1	0·2
3. Textiles			
Cotton Manufacturer	I	8	3·2
Woolcomber	III	1	
Dyer	III	1	
Mercer	II	1	
Tammy weaver	III	1	

Table 4.1   continued

Occupation/rank	Social class	No. of men	% of known total
4. *Professional*			
Clergy	I	8	3·8
Army	I	2	
Surgeon	I	2	
Solicitor	I	2	
5. *Retail*			
Grocer	II	4	3·0
Butcher	II	2	
Shopkeeper	II	2	
Innkeeper	II	1	
Apothecary	II	1	
Baker	II	1	
6. *Skilled manual and manual*[a]			
Woodman	IV	3	4·1
Ironmonger	III	2	
Goldsmith	III	2	
Watchmaker	III	1	
Engine builder	III	1	
Blacksmith	III	1	
Labourer	IV	1	
Carpenter	III	1	
Tanner	III	1	
Tallow chandler	III	1	
Cooper	II	1	
7. *Merchants and bankers*			
Merchant	I	8	2·7
Banker	I	2	
Known total		370	100·0

Table 4.1   continued

	Social class	%
percentage of known total	I	72 or 76
in each social class	II	16 or 11
	III	11
	IV	1

Note

[a] In principle, occupants of many of these ranks might be class II or class III, depending on status as employee or employer. Incidental information indicated that in the majority of cases the latter applied.

This corresponds to the classification of Wrightson and Levine, *Poverty and Piety*, p. 34, who place craftsmen in either class II or III on the basis of a wealth assessment; 'poor craftsmen' are categorised in class IV.

[b] Class I or II depending on extent of land owned.

Table 4.2   *Known occupations of the sough proprietors in the Wirksworth/Cromford region of Derbyshire, c. 1700–c. 1800*

Occupation/rank	Social class	No. of men
1. *Land*		
Gentry	I	31
Esquire	I	7
Yeoman	II	9
Farmer	I/II	6
Landowner	I	4
2. *Lead*		
Miner	III	14
Mineral agent	I	6
Lead merchant	I	6
Smelter	I	5

Table 4.2   continued

Occupation/rank	Social class	No. of men
3. *Textiles*		
Cotton manufacturer	I	4
Dyer	III	1
Mercer and draper	II	1
4. *Retail*		
Shopkeeper	II	1
Innkeeper	II	1
Grocer	II	1
Butcher	II	1
Apothecary	II	1
5 *Skilled manual*		
Goldsmith	III	2
Ironmonger	III	1
Tallow chandler	III	1
Banker	III	1
Tanner	III	1
Carpenter	III	1
Woodcutter	III	1
6. *Professional*		
Clergy	I	4
Surgeon	I	1
Army	I	1
7. *Miscellaneous*		
Merchant	I	4
Banker	I	2
Unknown		38
Known total		119

Table 4.2   continued

	Social class	%
percentage of known total	I	68 or 63
in each social class	II	13 or 18
	III	19
	IV	0

The capital invested in the region was of wide geographical origin, a feature that became increasingly evident as the eighteenth century progressed. Finance from outside the area was particularly important in Cromford sough, one of the most extensive enterprises in the area. Partners in this sough included two London merchants, a Sheffield banker and a Hertfordshire farmer, each of whom had additional local connections.

A small but significant change in the social and occupational profile of the Wirksworth/Cromford soughs is apparent during the period encompassed by this study. Late in the seventeenth century the backgrounds of the local sough investors exhibited a clear bias towards agricultural pursuits, whereas lead smelters had become more important by the early eighteenth century. The lead merchants and small businessmen predominated during the remainder of the century, and, in the nineteenth, landowners once again constituted the majority of investors.

There was a consistency in the pattern of ownership of the soughs in the Eyam area, and the majority of proprietors diversified their investments (Table 4.3). Land and lead occupational backgrounds constituted 55 and 25 per cent respectively of the total, the remainder being composed largely of retailers, husbandmen and miners.[3] Ten per cent of the enterprise was provided by individuals from class III and IV backgrounds, and possibly as much as 22 per cent was recruited from men of class II origin.[4] These figures, however, obscure the fact that most of the individuals in the more modest groups were proprietors in one sough enterprise only, whereas the more affluent gentry, lead merchants or smelters invested in several ventures. For the purposes of the study, however, the latter are counted only once. As a result, a random sample of the Eyam soughs would indicate the ratio of individuals from class I to those in II, III and IV to be greater than the figures suggest. The method was designed to create the most favourable statistical conditions for the emergence of the small man and indications of upward mobility.[5]

Table 4.3   *Known occupations of the sough proprietors in the Eyam/Calver region of Derbyshire, c. 1700–c. 1800*

Occupation/rank	Social class	No. of men
1. Land		
Gentry	I	26
Yeoman	II	14
Esquire	I	6
Landowner	I	3
Farmer	I/II	3
Husbandman	III	2
2. Lead		
Smelter	I	13
Lead merchant	I	5
Miner	III	5
Mine overseer	I	1
3. Textiles		
Cotton manufacturer	I	2
Woolcomber	III	1
4. Skilled manual		
Watchmaker	II	1
Engine builder	II	1
Blacksmith	III	1
5. Retail		
Grocer	II	2

Table 4.3   continued

Occupation/rank	Social class	No. of men
6. *Professional*		
Clergy	I	4
Army	I	1
7. *Miscellaneous*		
Merchant	I	3
Corn miller	I	1
Labourer	IV	1
Unknown		59
Known total		96

	Social class	%
percentage of known total	I	68 or 71
in each social class	II	22 or 19
	III	9
	IV	1

The impression gained, nevertheless, is of a greater affluence among the Eyam proprietors than among those in Wirksworth,[6] though the activities of the men of class III and class IV backgrounds in both areas were short-lived. With only two instances of long-distance infusion of capital,[7] investment in the Eyam soughs was more consistently local than in those in Wirksworth.[8]

Investors in the Youlgreave soughs were mostly landowners, lead merchants or smelters (Table 4.4). As in other areas, class I individuals predominated, and only 11 per cent[9] of the investors had class III or class IV origins. The region thus held limited attraction for the capital of the small man, even though it was rich in mineral, and investment was less likely to be the gamble typical of other parts of Derbyshire. The scale of enterprise in Youlgreave, however, was great and required a lengthy period of driving. The construction of

Table 4.4 *Known occupations of the sough proprietors in the Youlgreave/Alport region of Derbyshire, c. 1700–c. 1800*

Occupation/rank	Social class	No. of men
1. Land		
Gentry	I	10
Landowner	I	3
Esquire	I	1
Farmer	I/II	1
Yeoman	II	1
2. Lead		
Lead merchant	I	4
Miner	III	3
Smelter	I	4
Mine agent	I	1
Miner owner	I	2
3. Professional		
Solicitor	I	1
Surgeon	I	1
4. Manual		
Woodman	IV	1
5. Miscellaneous		
Merchant	I	1
Cotton manufacturer	I	1
Unknown		10
Known total		35

	Social class	%
percentage of known total	I	86 or 83
in each social class	II	3 or 6
	III	8
	IV	3

Table 4.5 *Known occupations of the sough proprietors in the Castleton region of Derbyshire, c. 1700–c. 1800*

Occupation/rank	Social class	No. of men
1. *Land*		
Gentry	I	6
Landowner	I/II	2
Esquire	I	1
Small farmer	III	2
Yeoman	II	1
2. *Lead*		
Lead merchant	I	1
Smelter	I	5
Miner	III	1
Barmaster	I	2
Mine owner	I	1
3. *Retail and manual*		
Butcher	II	1
Cooper	III	1
Unknown		2
Known total		24

	Social class	%
percentage of known total in each social class	I	75 or 67
	II	9 or 17
	III	17
	IV	0

Hillcarr sough, for instance, was started in 1766; it was driven four and a half miles over twenty-one years, at a cost of £32,000. Each partner invested £3,500, and it was not until 1787 that the reckoning book recorded any profit. The ore that the sough made accessible was rich and extensive, and for this reason the initial outlay was recouped within two years of completion. Hillcarr provides an example of the extent and the consequent expense of the soughs in the

area, which, together with the long gestation period before the initial
expenditure was covered, presumably deterred the man with limited
disposable capital resources.

The Castleton soughs (Table 4.5) were neither numerous nor
lucrative, and therefore offered few opportunities for upward social
mobility or long-term industrial leadership. With the exception of
Odin sough, which attracted investment from a socially diverse group
of people including a miner and a butcher, the proprietors of these
soughs were wealthy landowners, or individuals engaged in the lead
trade principally as merchants and smelters.

In the smaller areas (Tables 4.6–8) the social structure of
investment resembled the pattern within the soughs of the larger
areas. Members of the gentry and smelters comprised the largest
groups, while individuals from classes III and IV played no part,
except in the Taddington region, where the proportion of miner
investors was significant.

Table 4.6   *Known occupations of the sough proprietors in the Taddington*
            region of Derbyshire, c. 1700–c. 1800

Occupation/rank	Social class	No. of men
1. *Land*		
Gentry	I	7
Yeoman	II	2
Esquire	I	4
Farmer	I/II	3
Husbandman	III	1
2. *Lead*		
Smelter	I	7
Lead merchant	I	6
Miner	III	5
Mine owner	I	3
Mineral agent	I	2
Barmaster	I	1
3. *Skilled manual/retail*		
Ironmonger	II	1

Table 4.6   continued

Occupation/rank	Social class	No. of men
Woodman	III	1
Miscellaneous retail	II	1
4. *Textiles*		
Cotton manufacturer	I	1
Unknown		4
Known total		45

	Social class	%
percentage of known total in	I	76 or 69
each social class	II	9 or 16
	III	16
	IV	0

Table 4.7   *Known occupations of the sough proprietors in the Monyash region of Derbyshire, c. 1700–c. 1800*

Occupation/rank	Social class	No. of men
1. *Land*		
Gentry	I	4
Farmer	I/II	2
Esquire	I	1
2. *Lead*		
Smelter	I	4
Steward	I	2
Mine owner	I	1
Lead merchant	I	1
3. *Professional*		
Lawyer	I	1

Table 4.7   continued

Occupation/rank	Social class	No. of men
Unknown		5
Known total		16

	Social class	%
percentage of known total in	I	88 or 100
each social class	II	12 or 0
	III	0
	IV	0

Table 4.8   *Known occupations of the sough proprietors in the Winster region of Derbyshire, c. 1700–c. 1800*

Occupation/rank	Social class	No. of men
1. *Land*		
Gentry	I	17
Yeoman	II	3
2. *Lead*		
Smelter	I	4
Lead merchant	I	1
3. *Textile*		
Mercer	I	1
Unknown		6
Known total		26

	Social class	%
percentage of known total in	I	88
each social class	II	12
	III	0
	IV	0

In common with many industries of the period, the working capital requirements of lead mining, and particularly sough driving, were considerably larger than those of initial fixed capital inputs. Moreover the time lag between decisions to build and profits inevitably led to financial strain for investors, except for those with substantial capital resources. This situation minimised the potential opportunities for the small investor, certainly in the long term, unless he had credit facilities, which in the lead-mining industry were virtually impossible to obtain because of its speculative nature. Initial capital investment, however, could be small, so the emergence, if not the permanence, of the small man was possible. No systematic data exist on the size of stake, but such evidence as is available illustrates its great variation.[10] The mean stake, with large dispersion, lay between £20 and £40, an amount significantly less than that required for establishment in many contemporary industries.[11]

Although very small proportions were common, a one-twenty-fourth share was a typical holding. In a large sough, with a total investment of £15,600, this would represent £650; in a medium-sized sough, like those on Eyam edge, a one-twenty-fourth share cost between £50 and £150, while in the smallest sough encountered (Cowclose) the total investment was £120; a one-twenty-fourth share, therefore, £5.

At the other end of the scale were men such as John Spencer and Twigg, whose investments in the 1780s totalled over £5,000 and £7,415 respectively, amounts which would have enabled them to become established in cotton spinning on a large scale. Although there were very many small investors, middle-sized shareholders, such as those who held a one-twenty-fourth share in, say, three soughs on Eyam Great Vein, played a major role. Investment in this case would be in the region of £200 – £250, sufficient to become established as a modest brewer.

It is clear that the men who invested in the soughs and mines of the Derbyshire lead field were different, in terms of activity, from other contemporary industrial entrepreneurs. Although investment was an entrepreneurial function, the majority of sough proprietors did not perform such duties as organising production and marketing. The provision of fixed and working capital, and the receipt of cash or mineral if the enterprise were successful, constituted the main active role of the sough masters. Sough-driving operations required management and accounting skills, but these functions were performed either by an agent or by a small number of investors who were not heavily committed elsewhere. The remaining proprietors may be regarded as sleeping partners.

Because the maintenance and organisation of a sough provided insufficient employment for the entire group of partners, the majority of proprietors were able to engage simultaneously in other, often complementary, occupations. This diversification of activity was desirable because of the unpredictability of the profits from a sough. Before investing in soughs, many proprietors were already engaged elsewhere in the lead industry as agents, merchants or smelters, or a combination of these. Investment in mines and soughs was thus a logical step in the development of their original interest, as it facilitated supply of the raw material. Other investors, however, in order to maximise gain from an interest in mine and sough development, established themselves subsequently as lead merchants and smelters.

Large landowners, gentry and farmers, who perceived the new field of enterprise as a potentially lucrative outlet for surplus funds, also invested substantially in sough construction. They anticipated that this would lead to an increase in wealth and land-holding, together with an improvement in social status and a consolidation of their local power position. Rarely, however, was a change in social class achieved by this means; rather, it might facilitate a small upward shift within a status group.

The final important group of investors, the local retailers or small businessmen, were in a position to benefit directly or indirectly from their subsidiary interest. If fortunate, their investment in soughs would yield a profit which might then be reinvested in either of the enterprises. Moreover, if a district was found to be rich in mineral, then capital attracted from outside the locality would augment the growth of internal capital. The district would therefore prosper, as would the retailers in it. An expansion of local spending power and a rise in the demand for consumer goods would result, particularly for those articles on which lead mining depended, such as tools, ropes and candles. Inns, above all, thrived in the lead-mining district, as beer constituted one of the major items of a miner's expenditure.

The small proportion of class III and class IV investors requires comment. Only 12 per cent[12] of the eighteenth-century Derbyshire sough masters had origins within these categories, of whom slightly less than half were miners. The remainder comprised skilled manual workers (4·1 per cent of the total sample), textile workers (1 per cent) and agricultural labourers (1 per cent); the proportion was reasonably constant in each area. Initial capital investment in a sough was within the capacity of an individual of small means, but the subsequent demands of working capital may have deterred the small man from becoming involved, or resulted in his speedy failure if he did so.

The results of sough driving were less tangible than those of lead mining itself, and although the gains were potentially greater in the former activity, profits were often slow to emerge. The man of small means naturally required a speedy return on his investment in order to survive. The constant demand for capital from a sough enterprise quickly exhausted his limited savings. In principle, therefore, it can be argued that it was subsequent working capital requirements rather than initial capital investment that acted as a barrier to the long-term success of the man from a class III or class IV background.

The attraction of long-distance capital can be explained satisfactorily in terms of local connections. Twenty-seven of the 400 men in the sample of investors in the Derbyshire soughs came from far outside the region, and an additional thirty from the adjoining counties of Nottinghamshire, Staffordshire and Yorkshire. Evidence suggests that social, business or family ties played a vital role in attracting external capital.

George Clay, for instance, a London merchant, was born into a Derbyshire family. His sister married David Gregory, a Wirksworth farmer and son of Benjamin Gregory, lead merchant and friend of Clay. By investing in soughs Clay retained links with his native county and with lead mining.[13] Robert Dale, a London grocer, was born in Parwich, Derbyshire, the son of Robert Dale, a gentleman with lead-mining interests.[14] Likewise, John Heaton, a 'gentleman' of Westminster, and one of the Cromford sough proprietors in 1790, was originally a Derbyshire man and retained his 'second home' at Chatsworth.[15] Charles Roe, the son of a Parwich yeoman, became a man of diverse business interests, the most notable of which was a copper and brass manufactory at Eaton and Bosely, between Macclesfield and Congleton in Cheshire. Roe also owned the Penrhyn Du mine in Caernarvonshire and was instrumental in the development of the famous copper mine in Anglesey.[16] He subsequently became a lead merchant and invested heavily in the soughs of Eyam Edge.[17]

Thomas Spencer and his son John were members of the large and illustrious Spencer family of Cannon Hall, Barnsley. Previously they had resided at Middleton in Derbyshire and formed links there through marriage with the Simpsons, a formidable local mining family.[18] Another connection between this family and Derbyshire lead mining was created on the marriage of John Spencer to Christina, the daughter of Benjamin Ashton of Hathersage, a man with substantial assets in the mid-eighteenth-century lead industry.[19] Ashton, in turn, was related to the Bagshaws, also considerable sough investors, through Richard.[20]

The phenomenon of migration of capital can therefore be largely understood with reference to family and social bonds. Where social contacts did not exist, as in the cases of some London merchants, business associations formed the link. Henry Dickinson, for example, a merchant operating at East India House, London, was probably an agent or intermediary for one of the Derbyshire lead merchants in his export business. It seems that Dickinson assessed the gains to be made in Derbyshire lead mining, and, in order to share in them, diverted some of his capital to the field. His interest was short-lived, however, probably because of the insufficient return on his investment.[21]

The activities of the other London merchants, such as John Heathcote, whose brother lived in Bakewell, followed a similar pattern.[22] It is unlikely that the motives of these individuals were as extreme as those of Francis Gell, originally a London lead merchant who moved to Derbyshire in 1692 to begin driving Hannage sough, 'for the good of the local miners and the county as a whole'.[23]

It is clear that investment in the Derbyshire soughs constituted for many a subsidiary and often transient interest. As such it was a means to an end – an increase in wealth and possibly status[24] – rather than an end in itself. It thus differed from enterprises in other contemporary industries which typically required a full-time commitment. It was not only the sough proprietors and mine owners who engaged in other activities which were sometimes, but not always, connected with lead mining; the practice was followed by the manual workers also. This suggests that, for many, lead mining was a potentially lucrative 'hobby' rather than a means of subsistence. Such were the fluctuations and instability of the industry generally, in addition to the uncertainties of individual mines, that it was in the interests of economic survival to have one or more additional incomes of a reliable nature.

In this and other respects the structure and organisation of lead mining, in both the early and later stages of development, resembled that of pre-modern or even proto-industry. Anthony Eaton, an Eyam miner, who invested in Ladywash sough, is an example of a working miner with a variety of occupations. His probate inventory indicates yeoman as well as lead mining-activities. At the time of his death he owned four horses valued at £10; two cows, £2; seventy-six sheep, £15 15s (£15·75), as well as hay to the value of £6.[25] Likewise, Job Spencer, a Wirksworth miner, owned two cows £4 10s (£4·50) and two pigs, £1 10s (£1·50).[26]

Domestic weaving, too, was a popular means of increasing income or of minimising the negative effects of an unpredictable income.[27] George Buxton, a Middleton miner and shareholder in Harda Head sough in Taddington, remained solvent by utilising three looms, a cow valued at £2 10s (£2·50) and corn and hay, £2 2s 6d (£2·12½).[28] It became clear from an examination of the available inventories that those working miners who invested in soughs were not representative of the total population of miners. For this reason the individuals described as miner/investor in this study were deemed to belong to class III, unless additional information indicated this to be inappropriate, in which case an alternative category was used.[29]

The hypothesis that a relationship existed between the size of a sough and its social structure of investment, and that the smaller enterprises particularly would attract the savings of the man of limited means, has found support. Those individuals from class III and class IV backgrounds who emerged in the sample did invest in the smaller soughs. The quantity of capital invested in this type of sough was typically modest, and the return on it was unlikely to transform an individual's living standard or social status.[30] Fortunes acquired solely through sough investment were extremely rare, particularly if the investment were limited to one sough.[31] If, however, the return on the investment was sizeable, as was possible, it would increase the amount of capital available, and thus provide the opportunity for investment in additional and more extensive enterprises. This mechanism, however, operated most effectively for those individuals who initially possessed a moderate, rather than a small, stock of capital.

It follows that the larger soughs[32] were more expensive to drive, but they were usually successful in the long term, and the profit that accrued to each partner was proportionately greater than in the smaller ones. The gains, however, were rarely enormous. Occasionally, during the course of driving, soughers unearthed rich veins of lead worth thousands of pounds, but this occurred only in soughs driven over long distances, of which there were few.[33]

Investment in the lead mines and soughs was a gamble. Proceeds could be great; equally, they could be negligible or non-existent. As a result the richer men, who, as the tables indicate, constituted the majority of investors, tended to hold shares in a large number of enterprises in order to minimise the risk and maximise the gain.[34] The partnership of Barker and Wilkinson provides the clearest illustration of this practice. In 1762 they held shares in thirty-nine mines and soughs, twenty-three of which suffered a loss, while the remaining sixteen enjoyed a profit. The total capital lost in that year amounted to £160 8s 4½d (£160·42), which was more than compensated for by the £865 2s 9¾d (£865·14) profit made by the sixteen successes.[35]

Hence it was these individuals, with the most capital, who were in the strongest position to improve their social status. Individuals from classes III and IV could not afford to diversify their interests in this way, so unless they were extremely fortunate the chances of achieving substantial gains were small. The element of uncertainty, compounded by the heavy and unpredictable demands of working capital, effectively precluded the long-term success of the small man. A number of miner-investors' inventories and wills provide evidence that few fortunes were made and that upward mobility from classes III and IV was very unusual. It is, however, possible that some short-range mobility took place, in the sense that individuals, particularly in the higher social groups, passed between niches in the same category. Any mobility that did take place from the lower end of the social spectrum was likely to be precarious and typically short-term.

On the basis of the sample chosen for the purposes of this study, the conclusion is that only those who were fairly substantial in financial terms,[36] prior to investing in soughs, were in a position to achieve any lasting upward mobility through activities in the lead-mining industry. Also significant is the existence of a more diverse social structure of investment in the early part of the period *c.* 1700, when the activity of men of limited means was greater. This suggests that those individuals who entered the industry early in its development, before it became overloaded with hopeful entrepreneurs, had the greatest chance of survival and success. Working capital pressures were substantial at the beginning of the eighteenth century, just as they were subsequently, but because the gains were more easily obtained, and were shared among a comparatively small number of investors, a rise in social status for the man of limited means was at least possible. The subsequent boom in industry, and the small amount of capital required to become a shareholder, aroused the interest of such large numbers of men that it reduced the chance of any one of them of changing his social status. It was thus possible to improve oneself materially but only rarely to the extent of changing, in the long term, one's position in society, or of moving from class III or IV to a permanent position of industrial leadership.

These results, if they have general application, suggest that the early industrial leadership was composed largely of previous élite groups. While a small proportion had more lowly origins, their participation was temporary and, from their own point of view, unsuccessful. That is, while collectively they may have made a valuable contribution to the industry, they themselves enjoyed negligible gains.

It might be argued that sough driving involved a higher degree of risk than other industrial activities; and in other respects, such as capital investment, was not typical. Therefore generalisations drawn from an examination of this industry must be tentative, and will now be checked by a study of the leadership of the early cotton-spinning industry.

Notes

1   For comparative purposes the Derbyshire mining field was broken down into its major areas on the basis of documentary evidence, as follows:

    (a) *Wirksworth/Cromford:* an area rich in mineral resources, excavated for 2,000 years.

    (b) *Eyam/Calver:* included many of the smaller soughs of the type that drained a single mine, most within the Eyam Great Vein complex.

    (c) *Alport and Youlgreave:* a small area worked extensively until water hampered excavations, whereupon many miles of soughs were driven.

    (d) *Castleton:* an area rich in a variety of mineral especially Blue John fluorspar, but not outstanding for its numerous soughs.

    (e) Taddington ⎫

    (f) Monyash   ⎬   Smaller-scale constructions

    (g) Winster   ⎭

2   See Chapter II for elucidation of this.

3   Who presumably experienced some upward social mobility, in the short term at least, by this means.

4   Though some of these, particularly the farmers, might be class I.

5   Evidence of the bias favouring the lower social groups emerged from the list of investors in the Eyam area. Only 39 of the 540 names, with some duplication in the higher social groups from which individuals tended to invest in more than one enterprise, were men from class III or IV origins, representing only 5·4 per cent of the total.

6 Taking classes I and II together the proportion is greater in Eyam than in Wirksworth.

7 Sir Archibald Grant of Monymusk, Aberdeenshire, a partner in the Scotch mines company who subsequently strengthened his personal and business links with the area, and William Hearne, a London merchant.

8 Particularly Meerbrook and Cromford (Long) sough in which more than 50 per cent of the investors inhabited areas outside Derbyshire.

9 Or four thirty-fifths.

10 Some detail on this is presented in Chapter III, and Appendix I.

11 Brewing and cotton, for instance; see Chapter III, n. 56.

12 This is an 'upper bound' figure. The significance of bias is discussed in Chapter II, and above, n. 5.

13 Woolley mss 6680, D.R.O.

14 Devonshire Papers 131/11 Chatsworth House; Ince, *Pedigrees*, p. 202.

15 Deeds 913 (1787), 4404, 4407 (1794), D.P.L.

16 J. N. Rhodes, 'Derbyshire influences on lead mining in North Wales in the seventeenth and eighteenth centuries', *Bulletin of the Peak District Mines Historical Society*, III, 1968, pp. 345–7; and Charles Hadfield, *Canals of North West England*, vol. 1, 1970, p. 31 n.

17 Ince, *Pedigrees*, pp. 38 and 67.

18 Woolley mss 6680, f. 95, D.R.O.; and information supplied by J. H. Rieuwerts.

19 S. C. Newton, 'The Derbyshire gentry in the seventeenth century', *Derbyshire Archaeological Journal*, LXXXVI, 1966, p. 10.

20 Bagshaw Collection 13/3/350, 13/3/354, J.R.L.

21 5272/23 D.R.O.

22 Bagshaw Collection 448, S.C.L.

23 Woolley mss 6680, ff. 12–15, D.R.O.; and William Woolley *The History of the County of Derby*, 1712, f. 33420, D.P.L.

24 Achieved by expanding a land holding or by diverting capital into another status-rich activity such as banking.

25 Inventory of Anthony Eaton, 22 April 1736, L.J.R.O.

26 Inventory of Job Spencer, 21 April 1742, L.J.R.O.

27 Indicated by the inventories, where looms featured prominently.

28 Inventory of George Buxton, 19 April 1743, L.J.R.O.

29 Usually class IV, but very occasionally class II.

30 This reinforces the view that money begets money, and that a small capital grows disproportionately more slowly.

31 Which was the case in the activities of most small men.
32 Stoke, Cromford, Magclough, for instance.
33 Such as Hillcarr.
34 See Appendix I.
35 Barker and Wilkinson's shares, 1762, Bagshaw Collection 431a
     S.C.L.; and Appendix I.
36 At least class II.

V

The early cotton spinners:
(I) 1787

During the early period of the cotton industry's development three discrete technical spinning processes were available, each requiring different organisational methods and levels of capital investment. The jenny and the mule could be worked equally in a workshop or a factory, while the water frame, because of the stipulations of Arkwright's patent, necessitated a large production unit and a commensurately greater outlay on fixed capital. Factories built specially to house these technologies were unusual in the early stages of the industry, and it was apparently common to adapt old buildings, sometimes mills which had been employed for a different purpose, into spinning mills and warehouses.[1]

During the period 1780–1825, then, cotton factories varied not only in scale but also in type. S. D. Chapman has identified what he sees as the three main types.[2] The Type A mill was a small-scale operation, often employing hand-operated jennies or mules and possibly horse capstans for driving carding machines. The cost of establishing and equipping this type of mill was about £1,000–£2,000. The Type B factory was more often purpose-built and comprised three or four storeys. It came in two sizes: one designed to hold approximately 1,000 spindles and requiring up to £3,000 investment; and one at least twice as large with up to 3,000 spindles, costing from £5,000. These are often referred to as Arkwright-type mills. Type C was larger, generally steam-powered, and cost about £10,000. This category of mill was not usual until the early nineteenth century.

Clearly, there were big mills and small mills, and in each case it was possible – indeed, usual – to extend buildings and acquire additional machinery at any time after establishment. It would be impossible for an individual of small means, without a wealthy partner, to begin cotton production with a fixed capital investment on the scale outlined above. There were, however, ways in which he might obtain the minimum capital required for a smaller enterprise and expand subsequently through the practice of retaining profits. Even those who initially had access to more substantial sums might expand in the same way. From information available on profit levels, it is clear that capital accumulation through this process could, in principle, be rapid before 1815, and especially during the period of the Napoleonic wars.

The business records of M'Connel and Kennedy, for example, show a very high rate of profit in relation to capital in the period 1798–1808. From 1799 and 1804, in all but one year, the level of profits remained between 26·5 and 30 per cent of total capital, though it fell to between 10 and 15·3 per cent in the years 1804–08.[3] Although it can be argued that M'Connel and Kennedy were exceptional, their experience at least illustrates a general trend. 'Other evidence supports the view that cotton spinning realised higher profits at the turn of the century, and indeed during the war period as a whole, than it did in the quarter-century after 1815. The gap between price levels for cotton and yarn prices narrows strikingly through the first half of the century.'[4]

Kirkman Finlay, giving evidence to the select committee of the Commons in 1833, stated that profits by that time were very moderate because of intensified competition in the industry, and he believed that the highest profits had been achieved in the early years of the century, especially in spinning, when competition was less intense and prices were much higher.[5] More recently both Crouzet and Cottrell have drawn from evidence relating to cotton and other industries that corroborates this view.[6]

It is apparent, however, that the early years of an enterprise could be a struggle, except of course, where the partners were men of ample means, and it was frequently several years before a factory became fully equipped and maximum production and profits were reached.[7]

As a result expansion was possible in the long term, but financial difficulties were not uncommon in the interim. This could clearly disadvantage the aspiring small man who did not have access to external resources. For a variety of reasons, however, it has been suggested that the early years of cotton factory production contained entrepreneurial opportunities for the man of limited means. It is frequently believed, moreover, that these opportunities existed only for a short time. Recent work by V. A. C. Gattrell, however, suggests that as late as the 1840s small men continued to enter the industry and in many cases found credit easier to obtain than in the previous period.[8] It is the purpose of what follows to assess the extent to which the small man grasped the opportunities open to him in the earlier stage.

This chapter focuses upon the 1787 cotton spinners operating on the Arkwright principle. At this time the industry, in its new form, was located primarily in the Lowlands of Scotland, Lancashire, Yorkshire, North Wales and the Midland counties of Nottinghamshire, Derbyshire and Staffordshire. In 1787 Patrick Colquhoun conducted a survey for political purposes and enumerated by area each extant Arkwright-type mill.[9] The total number of cotton spinning mills run by water power he estimated at 145 and the average cost of each at £5,000. The enumeration cannot be accepted without reservation, however, and the limitations of the findings have been extensively discussed. It was argued by Unwin that Colquhoun had strong motives for exaggerating the quantity of capital invested in the rising industry. 'He was endeavouring to make out a case, during a crisis that had interrupted a boom in the trade, for protection against Indian calicoes and muslins.'[10] Despite the fact that many of the mills were probably worth a good deal less than the suggested £5,000,[11] both Ure and Baines, nineteenth-century commentators on the cotton industry, accept as accurate the actual number of mills stated.[12] Allowing for the weaknesses in Colquhoun's work, which clearly relate to the value rather than the number of mills, it provides a useful basis from which to examine the origins of the leaders of the late eighteenth-century cotton industry. That is, it is sufficient to provide a sampling frame.[13]

The first objective of this section is to identify each of the mills distinguished in Colquhoun's survey, to ascertain its location and to name, as far as possible, all the partners involved in the enterprise. Secondly, an attempt is made to discover the occupational background of each entrepreneur, from which to make an assessment of the type of man who entered the industry at this early stage. The information acquired in this way is also used to test the central hypothesis that the early stages of transition to large-scale industry created unprecedented opportunities for upward social mobility.[14]

It is clear from the findings, presented here in a composite table (5.1), and by area, according to Colquhoun's survey, that internal capital played a vital role in the financing of the early cotton industry. In each area examined, hereditary leaders, who diverted capital into cotton from another branch of textile production, constituted the majority of entrepreneurs.

Table 5.1 *Occupational backgrounds of the 1787 factory owners in England and Wales*

Occupation/rank	Social class	No. of men
Textile trades		
Bleacher and dyer	II	4
Calico printer	II	13
Framework knitter	III	1
Fuller	II	1
Fustian manufacturer	II	22
Hosier	II	23
Mercer and draper	II	22
Merchant	I	30
Muslin manufacturer	II	3
Silk manufacturer	I	7
Stuff/wool manufacturer	II	8
Other textile manufacturer (e.g. check, hat)	II	27
Warehouseman/employee	IV	4
Non-textile trades		
Architect	I	1

Table 5.1   continued

Occupation/rank	Social class	No. of men
Banker	I	9
Brewer	I	8
Excise officer	I	1
Heiress	I	1
Ironmonger	II	1
Joiner	III	1
Land agent	I	1
Landowner/gentry	I	13
Landowner/yeoman or equivalent	II	3
Lawyer	I	1
Lead/iron manufacturer	I	3
London merchant	I	4
Machine maker/mechanic	III	8
Miller	I	6
Millwright	III	1
Paper manufacturer	I	2
Potter	II	1
Unknown		52
Total		282

	Social class	%
Percentage of known total in each social class	I	38
	II	56
	III	5
	IV	2

As early as 1787 the cotton industry was concentrated in Lancashire, where forty-three Arkwright-type mills were in production. The capital for the new industry was recruited almost entirely from local sources;[15] and the background of all the early Lancashire cotton spinners included in the survey involved some contact, direct or indirect, with the textile trade (Table 5.2).

Local directories for 1772 and 1781 indicate a predominance of

Table 5.2   *Occupational backgrounds of the 1787 factory owners in Lancashire*

Occupation/rank	Social class	No. of men
Textile trades		
Bleacher	II	1
Calico printer and manufacturer	II	10
Fustian manufacturer	II	16
Hosier	II	2
Linen draper	II	2
Merchant	I	15
Muslin manufacturer	II	3
Silk merchant and manufacturer	I	2
Other textile manufacturer (e.g. check, hat)	II	12
Warehouseman/employee	IV	2
Non-textile trades		
Banker	I	1
Brewer	I	2
Gentry/large landowner	I	2
Lawyer	I	1
Lead/iron manufacturer	I	1
Machine maker/mechanic	III	3
Unknown		17
Total		92
	Social class	%
Percentage of known total in each social class	I	29
	II	64
	III	4
	IV	3

former fustian manufacturers, including Horrocks and Ashworth, subsequent cotton spinning giants. The Peels and five other 1787 cotton spinners had accumulated capital as calico printers and manufacturers. The Philips family of Salford had owned three small factories,[16] manufacturing respectively smallware, silk and linen and hats, before concentrating on cotton spinning. Six 1787 manufacturers had previously been engaged as textile middlemen and merchants. Each of these cases indicated a moderate degree of upward mobility in the progression to cotton spinning, and each illustrated the role of either inherited wealth or, more important, capital accumulated in previous textile enterprises.

Samuel Withington and James Halliwell were examples of a different phenomenon. The original occupation of the former was that of warehouseman;[17] from there he progressed to smallware and thread manufacturer,[18] and finally to cotton spinner. The experience of James Halliwell illustrates a greater degree of mobility. He began work as a porter in the Peels' Manchester warehouse, and gained gradual but steady promotion, until he was offered a partnership in one of the Peels' Lancashire enterprises.[19]

Only a handful of the early Lancashire cotton spinners had previously been engaged in non-textile activities, and each of these had inherited or acquired wealth. John Parker, for instance, was a Clitheroe lawyer and banker and formed the firm of J. & J. Parker in the Clitheroe area with a relative, another John Parker, of Chancery Lane, London.[20] Abraham Clegg of Oldham came from a large land-owning family who were engaged in a cluster of business ventures.[21] The Simpson brothers who partnered Richard Arkwright junior and John Whittenbury in a Manchester mill came from a family with lead-mining interests.[22]

In terms of occupational backgrounds, the Derbyshire entrepreneurs were evenly split between textile and non-textile activities. In the former category, Table 5.3 illustrates the predominance of former hosiers. Two of these had benefited from the acquisition of lucrative connections. John Cooper[23] had married the sister of Jedediah Strutt, and Anthony Bradley cultivated the friendship of members of the local gentry, from whom he obtained essential financial assistance.[24] Land and lead mining formed the previous interest of most of the entrepreneurs in the non-textile category. Peter Nightingale retained his original occupation as lead

merchant after setting up as a cotton spinner,[25] and Thomas Evans
was a notable Derby banker in addition to owning lead and calamine
mines.[26] There was a close connection between banking and wealth
made in trade and industry. This relationship could operate in either
direction, but in any case was mutually reinforcing. Wealth made in
an industrial or commercial enterprise, for instance, could become the
basis for setting up as a banker; conversely the working capital or the

Table 5.3 *Occupational backgrounds of the 1787 factory owners in
Derbyshire*

Occupation/rank	Social class	No. of men
Textile trades		
Hosier (town)	II	3
Hosier (country)	II	3
Mercer and draper	II	3
Bleacher	II	1
Non-textile trades		
Large landowner	I	6
Lead manufacturer	I	1
Banker	I	1
Grazier	II*	2
Joiner	III	1
Unknown		9
Total		30
	Social class	%
Percentage of known total	I	38
in each social class	II	57
	III	5
	IV	0

*An adjustment of category was made here, as the evidence showed the
individuals concerned to be owners of some land.

bank deposits could establish, or sustain, an industrial business with longer-term credit.[27]

Most of the principal cotton spinners in Nottinghamshire had originally been involved in the hosiery industry, either as hosiers or as mercers. Former drapers comprised the other major group. Capital

Table 5.4　*Occupational backgrounds of the 1787 factory owners in Nottinghamshire*

Occupation/rank	Social class	No. of men
Textile trades		
Merchant	I	6
Silk manufacturer	I	3
Hosier (town)	II	5
Hosier (country)	II	2
Mercer and draper	II	5
Framework knitter	III	1
Non-textile trades		
Miller	I	2
Lead manufacturer	I	1
Large landowner	I	1
Architect	I	1
Brewer/publican	II	2
Potter	II	1
Machine maker/mechanic	III	4
Ironmonger	II	1
Unknown		1
Total		36
	Social class	*%*
Percentage of known total in each social class	I	40
	II	46
	III	14
	IV	0

from a variety of non-textile interests, as indicated in Table 5.4, established approximately forty per cent of the total firms in this area.

The predominance of hosiery interests in the Nottinghamshire and Derbyshire cotton enterprises corresponds to the importance of fustian manufacturers in the Lancashire cotton industry, and it appears that resources and factor inputs were transferred without difficulty.

In Staffordshire (Table 5.5) the cotton industry was dominated by the three enterprises of the Peel family.[28] Benjamin Wilson, a leading Burton brewer, provided much of the capital for the cotton mill that he worked with the Dickens brothers, who had previously been brewers, mercers, drapers and manufacturers.[29] This reflected the phenomenon of brewers diversifying their interests because of the shortness of the brewing season.[30]

Table 5.5   *Occupational backgrounds of the 1787 factory owners in Staffordshire*

Occupation/rank	Social class	No. of men
Textile trades		
Silk manufacturer	I	2
Calico printer	II	1
Non-textile trades		
Miller	I	2
Brewer	II	3
Grazier	II	1
Unknown		4
Total		13
	Social class	%
Percentage of known total in each social class	I	44
	II	56
	III	0
	IV	0

Table 5.6 *Occupational backgrounds of the 1787 factory owners in Yorkshire*

Occupation/rank	Social class	No. of men
Textile trades		
Calico printer	II	1
Cloth merchant	I	2
Draper	II	1
Hosier	II	4
Mercer	II	1
Shalloon manufacturer	II	1
Stuff/wool manufacturer	II	8
Non-textile trades		
Banker	I	3
Excise officer	I	1
Heiress	I	1
Land agent	I	1
Landowner/gentry	I	3
London merchant	I	2
Miller	I	2
Millwright	III	1
Unknown		5
Total		37
	Social class	%
Percentage of known total	I	44
in each social class	II	50
	III	6
	IV	0

In Yorkshire (Table 5.6) the cotton industry was clearly influenced by that in Lancashire.[31] The first cotton mill in the county, at Keighley, was established and run by George and William Clayton and Thomas Walshman, 'Gentlemen from Lancashire'.[32] Walshman was originally a partner with Arkwright, Strutt, Need and Cross in an early cotton enterprise near Chorley.[33] Most of those Yorkshire cotton spinners who had diverted capital from a previous textile occupation had been stuff (worsted) manufacturers, and converted their original premises for the purpose. After several years' activity in the cotton industry these individuals reverted to worsted manufacture as the regional specialisation and concentration of the two industries developed.[34] All those in the non-textile category were men of some substance. Many of them were landowners with no previous interest in textiles whose involvement in cotton spinning was short-lived.[35]

Table 5.7   *Occupational backgrounds of the 1787 factory owners in Flintshire*

Occupation/rank	Social class	No. of men
Textile trades		
Fustian manufacturer	II	3
Other textile trades	II	3
Non-textile trades		
Liquor merchant	II	1
Diverse business interests	II	1
Machine maker	III	1
Unknown		0
Total		9
	Social class	%
Percentage of known total	I	0
in each social class	II	89
	III	11
	IV	0

The majority of the remaining principal cotton spinners in England and Wales had backgrounds in, or connected with, the textile industry. The Flintshire mills (Table 5.7) require particular comment. In 1787 the three mills in the region were owned by the Holywell Twist Company,[36] in which there was a strong Lancashire interest and a rapid turnover of partners. At the time of Colquhoun's survey, those involved were Peter Atherton,[37] a Manchester machine builder, to whom Arkwright had applied for financial assistance in his early struggling days; several fustian manufacturers;[38] and the Dumbells, a family of unspecified textile manufacturers from Warrington.[39] Most of these partners were concomitantly engaged in cotton spinning in Lancashire and ultimately withdrew their interest from the Flintshire enterprise.

The results from the peripheral areas of cotton manufacture, presented in Tables 5.8 and 5.9, conform to the pattern established in the core areas; that is, the overwhelming proportion of 1787 entrepreneurs had reasonably high-status textile backgrounds.

The results presented in the tables illustrate clearly the strength of hereditary leadership. Between 75 and 80 per cent of the early cotton spinners had previously been engaged in textiles. This supports the view that transference of resources into the new process of large-scale cotton manufacture was an apparently simple matter and clearly an attractive proposition. The mechanics of diverting resources in this way have not been adequately examined, but the action can be explained in terms of financial gain. Most of the individuals in this category had been workshop owners of moderate success. The emergence of the cotton industry towards the end of the eighteenth century indicated the imminent contraction of the traditional local textile production for which, in any case, the market was limited. As a result, on the basis of economic rationality, the only option likely to meet with long-term success was a shift into the large-scale and growing cotton industry, where potentially great gains were to be made.

The results also indicate that the small man in terms of capital accummulation was not a common feature of the early cotton-spinning industry. There are several plausible explanations. It is possible that, contrary to popular belief, developments in the cotton industry late in the eighteenth century did not provide unprecedented opportunities for the small man. Alternatively, the man of limited means chose to ignore such opportunities as did exist. It is also possible that attempts to enter the cotton industry in an

Table 5.8   *Occupational backgrounds of the 1787 factory owners in Cumberland and Westmorland*

Occupation/rank	Social class	No. of men
Textile trades		
Calico printer	II	1
Check manufacturer	II	1
Dyer	II	1
Fuller	II	1
Fustian manufacturer	II	3
Hosier	II	1
Mercer	II	1
Merchant	I	2
Other textile manufacturer	II	4
Warehouseman	IV	1
Non-textile trades		
Banker	I	2
Paper maker	I	1
Unknown		11
Total		30

	Social class	%
Percentage of known total	I	26
in each social class	II	68
	III	0
	IV	6

entrepreneurial capacity were made by small men, but unanticipated barriers were encountered leading to their rapid demise. Whatever the explanation, the most reasonable conclusion to draw from the evidence is that for men of moderate wealth the 'new' cotton industry clearly provided a means by which this wealth might be increased and the status of the individual improved. In terms of the classification employed here,[40] most of the 1787 cotton spinners had emerged from classes I and II, and were thus already possessed of some property

Table 5.9 *Occupational background of the 1787 factory owners elsewhere in England and Wales (Berkshire, Cheshire, Gloucestershire, Pembrokeshire, Worcestershire)*

Occupation/rank	Social class	No. of men
Textile trades		
Bleacher	II	1
Hosier	II	3
Mercer and draper	II	9
Merchant	I	5
Textile manufacturer (check, wool)	II	6
Warehouseman	IV	1
Non-textile trades		
Banker	I	1
Landowner	I	1
London merchant	I	2
Paper manufacturer	I	1
Unknown		9
Total		39
	Social class	%
Percentage of known total in each social class	I	33
	II	63
	III	0
	IV	4

and status.

The men of humbler origins who successfully became cotton spinners provide an interesting study. James Halliwell and James Yates achieved this position through internal promotion in the enterprise of the well established Peel family.[41] Halliwell was initially a porter in the Peels' warehouse at Manchester, gained recognition from his employers, and was appointed packer, then traveller, and penultimately promoted to agent at the Cannon Street warehouse. It was apparently because of his dedication and manifest managerial talents that Halliwell was finally offered a partnership in the Peels' Bolton, Bury and Holcombe concerns.[42] James Yates, originally a cotton mill apprentice, followed a similar route and became a partner in one of the Peel enterprises, with a modest capital contribution of £200.[43]

Richard Arkwright was clearly enterprising, though the extent of the poverty of his background has probably been exaggerated. He appears to have cultivated lucrative connections without too much difficulty, but in this respect he was exceptional and particularly fortunate.[44] The other apparently humble individuals were also fortunate or unusual in some way. Thomas James, for instance, was a framesmith; he came from a family of brickmakers[45] and was the Nottingham partner of James Hargreaves, a modest hand-loom weaver. James was not typical of his class, however, as he was able to raise capital for his mill from his family's holding of land.[46] Also unusual were Abraham Flint, a small grazier, who 'happened' to have a fast-flowing stream running through his upland pastures,[47] and Thomas Parkes, a plumber and grazier of Staffordshire, a member of whose family owned land through which the Tean brook meandered.[48]

Some explanation of the emerging pattern is required. The hereditary leaders who predominated typically possessed 'modest' fortunes, that is, wealth approaching several hundred pounds. This accumulated capital was useful but generally insufficient to finance the working, in addition to the building, of an Arkwright-type mill. As a result, one or more partners with the necessary capital were often acquired.

The Peels, like many early entrepreneurs, experienced early difficulties in recruiting capital, particularly working capital, and to overcome the problem they encouraged individuals, such as James Tipping, with capital and contacts to join them in partnership.[49] For similar reasons Peter Atherton built up a collection of partners. Initially he enlisted the help of William Harrison, a Manchester fustian manufacturer, and, later, J. & T. Hodgson, Liverpool merchants, to tide him over his difficulties.[50] Later, as a result of unanticipated costs, Christopher Smalley attracted William Douglas and other Lancashire merchants to Holywell.[51] It was necessary to choose partners with care, however, and trustworthiness and managerial skills were as important factors as capital. Subsequently, as the size of the business unit grew, the services of a good manager were crucial, and this development provided a mode of entry for talented men without capital.

Other areas of expertise such as mechanical skills were also seen to be a valuable asset, and an individual without wealth might be made a partner on the strength of them. Such was the case of James Greenwood, who was brought into the partnership of Watsons Blakey & Co. (Keighley) in 1784 because the other partners were in need of help with the building of the mill and machinery. In the partnership agreement it was stated that 'James Greenwood, not having at present any capital to bring into stock' is 'to be employed in the said concern' because he has 'a plan in respect of other mills of a similar nature to the intended one and a genius well adapted for constructing the machines and other works to be made use of and employed in an about the said intended mill.' In the long term, however, Greenwood was to make a financial contribution equivalent to that of the other partners. He was to be paid 13s 6d a week until his share of the profits amounted to a sum similar to that paid by the other partners; when he had established his capital in the firm he was to be paid interest on that amount.[52]

Where possible, partnerships were founded within the family network; acquired family connections, through marriage, often formed the basis of a successful business. In Derbyshire, for instance, the establishment of John Cooper's cotton mill closely followed his marriage into the Strutt family, and he soon obtained the services as partner of one Dale, a local landowner.[53] James Yates was also astute in his choice of wife. It was following his marriage to Robert Peel's daughter that he was made a partner, with a small capital contribution.[54]

Clearly marriage was a mechanism by which the humble individual might acquire useful connections; indeed, in many instances it was a calculated move on the part of the aspiring entrepreneur to seize a

share in the father-in-law's firm. This was explicitly the case in the
proposed match between Samuel Oldknow and Peter Drinkwater's
daughter. It was a blatant, but unsuccessful, attempt on the part of the
former to gain control of Drinkwater's establishment, and by this
means to further his own business enterprise.[55] The converse could
also apply, however. It is conceivable that, if the owner of the
business lacked a suitable son to maintain it, he might attempt to keep
it in the family by inducing his daughter to marry a good manager, or
by persuading a talented and trustworthy man to marry his
daughter.[56]

Three Nottinghamshire cotton spinners, all former hosiers, were
related by marriage. Samuel Unwin was joined in partnership in his
second mill by his son-in-law, James Heygate.[57] His other son-in-law,
John White, an enterprising hosier, owned a mill in Basford with
Robert Hall and his son.[58] William Stanford took as partner his son-
in-law, John Burnside, a Nottingham hosier, a step which aided the
expansion of his foundry and cotton mill on the river Mann at
Mansfield.[59]

The most successful of the early cotton spinners participated in
more than one partnership. The experience of Richard Arkwright
provides a remarkable example of this phenomenon. He initially
applied to Peter Atherton[60] for financial help in 1768, but had more
success with John Smalley, previously a liquor merchant and painter
of Preston.[61] Smalley became Arkwright's partner in mills at Preston
and Nottingham, and was probably manager of the Cromford mill.[62]
Smalley's resources ran out after a couple of years, whereupon
Arkwright borrowed from Wright's bank to relieve the liquidity
crisis. To resolve the longer-term prospect of capital shortage, he
persuaded Strutt and Need to join him in partnership.[63]

In addition to his interest in several cotton-spinning enterprises in
Nottinghamshire, Arkwright was one of the partners, together with
Strutt, Need, Walshman and Cross, in the ill-fated Birkacre factory
near Chorley.[64] Established in 1777, it was reputedly the first
Arkwright-type mill to be established outside the Midlands, but was
destroyed by mobs in 1780. In the mid-1780s Arkwright extended
his ventures to Scotland. Not only did he partner David Dale in

Scotland's first cotton mill at New Lanark, but he was also the inspiration behind the Buchanan's mill at Deanston. He then became Claude Alexander's partner at Catrine.[65]

Similarly, Peter Atherton, originally a machine builder in Warrington, diversified his business interests. By 1783 he was engaged in cotton spinning with William Douglas at Pendleton, near Manchester.[66] In 1787 he was attracted to Flintshire, where he became a partner in the Holywell Twist Company, which he subsequently took over.[67] He later developed merchanting interests at Liverpool and extended his Welsh connection by investing in a new cotton mill at Mold. During the 1790s he became a partner of Philips & Lee of Salford.[68]

The Clayton brothers and Thomas Walshman were participants in an interesting variety of partnerships. Together they were responsible for the establishment of Yorkshire's first cotton-spinning mill, at Keighley, and a second one at Langcliffe.[69] Walshman had previously been a partner at the Birkacre factory, and the Claytons, while retaining their Lancashire and Yorkshire contacts, diversified geographically by joining Gaskell in a cotton mill at Macclesfield.[70] This development was temporary, however, and early in the 1830s the family settled in Giggleswick, Lancashire.[71]

William Douglas, who partnered Peter Atherton in Manchester and Holywell, also joined Dale and McCaul in partnership in a cotton mill at Newton Stewart, Wigtownshire, in 1787.[72] It is clear that experienced English cotton spinners, particularly those with Lancashire connections, were instrumental in the establishment of the industry in Scotland. Further examples include Gideon Bickerdike, the Manchester merchant of Dutch extraction who was the principal partner at the Deanston cotton mill in Perthshire, and James Doxon, who in 1789 had interests in Manchester, Stockport and Glasgow.[73] In most cases, however, after an initial burst of enthusiasm, the English investors withdrew when the concentration of the cotton industry in the Lancashire area strengthened.

The practice of enlarging the range of partnerships did not necessarily require a large capital expenditure. In an enterprise financed by a number of partners the contribution of each could be modest. Moreover, by diversifying investments an individual was potentially maximising his return, or minimising the risk involved. The converse could equally apply however. At a time when each partner was legally responsible for the debts of the enterprise the multiplication of partnerships could conceivably have increased risk rather than reduced it.

The background and career of Sir Robert Peel have been well documented, and although, like Arkwright, neither he nor his activities were typical of contemporary businessmen, Peel is interesting in the way in which he, or his enterprises, apparently provided opportunities for employees to take a financial interest in the business, or to branch out on their own. Before 1760 the partnership of Peel, Howarth and Yates was formed at Church, Blackburn, and, like many subsequent partners, the Howarths soon took their capital and their interest elsewhere. By 1784 the Peels had started works in Burton, Bolton and Warrington, and their policy of promoting competent and trustworthy employees was originally necessitated by the sheer extent and diversity of the concerns.[74] The majority of those promoted in this way appear to have viewed internal movement as a step towards an independent business career.

Henry Warren, for instance, was promoted to a partnership at Holcombe, and subsequently established his own firm with John Roberts, himself a former employee of the Peels.[75] Warren had been an engraver at Peel & Yates's Bury works, and was promoted to senior partner at the Peels' Tamworth works. Robert Duck and Charles Pott had been 'servants' of Sir Robert Peel and left in 1792 to open a mill together in Manchester. Richard Thompson, at one time superintendent of Peel's cotton mill, moved on to establish his own mill at Newcastle under Lyme.[76] These are clear signs of upward mobility, but unfortunately no evidence is available to indicate the longevity or degree of success of the individuals and their enterprises.

This chapter has been concerned with an analysis of the social profile of firms engaged in early Arkwright-type cotton spinning. Arkwright mills were the largest units of production at this time, and could entail substantial capital outlay. It has frequently been claimed that 'artisan' capital made an important contribution to the establishment of the new type and scale of enterprise. The results, however, suggest that the man with limited initial capital did not play a major role. It is argued below that, despite the mechanisms available for capital economising, anything else would have been surprising.

Much work on the early cotton industry has stressed the predominance of internal sources of capital.[77] Crouzet, for instance, has noted that a large number of enterprises of the second half of the eighteenth century were founded by profits from production at the artisan level. He also argues that the role of artisan capital fell as technological progress raised the threshold of entry into factory production.[78] There were several possible methods of minimising initial fixed capital costs in the early period of factory industry, which, in principle, facilitated the emergence of the small man. The most common was to acquire and adapt second-hand buildings. In fact it was rare to start a business with a large new mill, complete with machinery. The process of adapting or renting second-hand buildings was facilitated by the existence, in many rising commercial localities, of a flourishing local property market for renting industrial buildings which enabled aspiring industrialists to reserve their savings for working capital. The larger, purpose-built mill tended to be constructed from accumulated profits after some years, once business had become well established, and was only gradually equipped with machinery, often second-hand.[79]

It has been argued that it was relatively simple and inexpensive to transfer mills, workshops, warehouses and machinery from other industries to cotton,[80] and this clearly occurred on a large scale. In Stockport, for instance, most of the town's silk mills had been converted to cotton spinning by the late 1780s,[81] and equivalent processes were observed in Staffordshire and Nottinghamshire.[82] In some areas, however, the transition to cotton spinning, particularly from other textile uses, was only temporary, and notably in the West Riding and in Stockport, worsted and silk production soon came to predominate once more. Many water mills were transformed from non-textile use. Corn mills, paper mills, iron and lead works were reorganised and re-equipped for cotton spinning, and this often represented a shift of capital away from an industry that was declining locally.[83] The switch was not universally feasible, as a near-by river or fast-flowing stream was desirable in order to exploit the water power for the new types of machinery. This and other factors led to the emergence of a trend for mills, particularly of the Arkwright variety, to be built in isolated rural areas. Arkwright himself initiated the practice by establishing works and a new community in Cromford, and his example was followed by many others, such as Greg at Styal[84] and Needham at Litton.[85] In Scotland evidence indicates that the early cotton mills also conformed to this pattern.[86]

The ease of transition to cotton from other sectors of the textile industry, however, should not be exaggerated. It could be cheap and simple, but more often it was a complex and expensive process. Some of the technology used in an earlier stage of the industry had potential for adaptation, but generally, because of technical developments, it was necessary in the long term to invest in the latest purpose-designed technology. Warehouses were clearly transferable without complication, but the capital saving in this case was negligible.

The adoption of a moneyed partner could also ease the burden of capital-raising for the individual whose resources were small or limited. The procedure was employed by those not so restricted financially as well, but cautiously, as it was considered imprudent to trust an individual outside the family network. For other reasons, too, members of kinship groups were most likely candidates for partnership. Because of the joint-stock laws the importance of trust operated in both directions. That is, the potential partner had to be as convinced of the worthiness of future colleagues as they of him.

The method was adopted particularly in times of expansion, but the individual of humble means was in a weak position to form contacts that might lead to the discovery of an appropriate partner. In other words, the partnership system was, in principle, a means of minimising the capital that an individual needed to supply, but it was not a measure easily available to those who most needed it. There are, however, some instances in a variety of contemporary industries of young men with a limited quantity of capital persuading wealthy men to become partners, often in the 'sleeping' sense, and as a result being able subsequently to collect further capital by being personally backed by other creditors.[87] The major hurdle for the small man, therefore, was to obtain the initial moneyed partner; thereafter, creditors and additional partners were more readily acquired.

Nevertheless the expense involved in setting up as a cotton spinner was considerable, even allowing for these cost-reducing procedures. The demands of working capital, however, were more extensive, and frequently ruined the small man. Ways of overcoming the pressure of fixed capital costs existed, but the extent of working capital requirements were often unanticipated and were altogether more difficult to bear. The amount of fixed capital involved in the cotton industry, in relation to working capital, has often been exaggerated, but recent work indicates that the former was less, possibly substantially less, than the latter. In the typical up-to-date mill in the period 1780–1830 fixed capital is believed to have represented only just over half the capital invested.[88] S. D. Chapman calculates that until 1815 fixed capital costs in the cotton industry constituted only 25 per cent of the total.[89] Peter Mathias suggests that fixed assets were a smaller proportion still of total assets, and that assets requiring short-term credit were usually at least four or five times greater. To exacerbate the situation, the relative slowness of the distribution system in the eighteenth-century economy meant that a very high level of stocks had to be financed relative to turnover.[90]

As a result, the problem of acquiring capital was not only connected with the purchase of buildings and machinery but was more seriously centred on the search for working capital, for stocks of raw materials, work in progress and finished commodities, in addition to rents, interest and wage payments. This was a situation similar to that faced by the organisers of the putting-out system, and although the organisation of the industry had changed the system of financing it had not. This may partly explain why the origins of the new industrialists were so similar to those of the leaders of the domestic industry: it was these individuals who controlled the credit network.

The system of trade credit which facilitated the flow of working capital for the well established industrialist was simply not available to the new or struggling small man. Credit, to cover the expensive gap between sales and returns, was not easily obtained and had to be acquired gradually. Many of the problems experienced by the small man in this context were aggravated by what Mathias terms the 'sociological gap' between landed, commercial and professional wealth and the entrepreneur in a humble station in life without face-to-face contact.[91] An individual with limited means and limited contacts, faced with the unexpected burden of working capital costs, could not hope to be granted the credit he needed. Collateral and good local 'credit' were necessary. This obstacle would result in the demise of the new small firm unless there was alternative access to funds. The most common and important source of external funding, however, was the kinship network, which was unlikely to be fruitful for the man of humble origins.

It has been noted, however, that there was remarkable solidarity among competing cotton-spinning enterprises in this period, from which the small man might benefit. Both fixed and working capital was often raised from business contacts in the same industry. It was in their interest to help fellow traders, because they never knew when they too might need help. John Greenwood, of Keighley, for example, having profited from a cotton-spinning business, increased his wealth through lending to fellow traders.[92] Inter-firm credit, however, though generally a development stimulating the growth of the industry, could result in mass bankruptcy if one of the businesses in the relationship failed.

Moreover it seems that even where institutional credit facilities were available to the small man there might be drawbacks. Recently, for instance, S. D. Chapman has observed that even during the 1830s, a period of easy credit for all, such was the instability of individual banks that most entrepreneurs tried to keep their institutional borrowing to a minimum and to utilise other sources if at all possible.[93] This suggests that in the earlier period institutional forms of credit, if and when they were granted to the struggling small man, were quite likely to be more of a liability than a help. Nevertheless it is clear that even in the early stages of the cotton industry, when initial fixed capital requirements were lower than subsequently working capital pressures effectively reduced the chances of long-term success for the small man.

The evidence of our study indicates a predominance of merchant capital, if not mercantile activity, and a large-scale migration of capital from other spheres of the textile industry. More specifically, capital was recruited from fustian and calico manufacturers in Lancashire, from hosiers and to a lesser extent silk manufacturers in Nottinghamshire, Derbyshire and Staffordshire, and from the stuff and wool makers in Yorkshire. This illustrates the essential continuity of leadership that existed from domestic to factory-based production.

The expense involved in setting up as a cotton spinner, and maintaining that position, even allowing for transference of fixed capital from another industry, was great, and ultimately beyond the means of the individual artisan wage earner operating independently, however frugal and thrifty he might have been. The foregoing discussion has put forward the argument that the extent of working capital requirements and the difficulties involved in obtaining credit effectively precluded the long-term existence of the small man without good connections. It is hardly surprising, therefore, that most of the capital necessary for the new factory production came from the workshop-based textile sector, the remainder being diverted from land and mining enterprises. Most capital investment was recruited from local sources. London bankers and merchants provided a little, regarding the infant industry as a potentially lucrative outlet for their financial resources. Gideon Bickerdike from Holland,[94] and the French Salvin brothers,[95] provide the only instances of foreign capital.

This chapter has illustrated the importance of hereditary capital or the essential continuity of investment, and the proportionately small contribution of artisan capital. The individuals of humble origin who became successful did so, necessarily, through useful connections, fortunate encounters or internal promotion. Significantly, their success was short-term. Most of the early cotton spinners were men of modest or moderate capital[96] (56 per cent in class II) which under the circumstances is not surprising. The initial capital outlay necessary to purchase the modicum of machinery and building could be as little as several hundred pounds but the cost of raw materials, labour, and lags between sales and returns, required amounts beyond the reach of the man of small means and limited connections. It seems, therefore, that the opportunities available to the small man in the early years of the cotton industry were less extensive than is often suggested.

Notes

1 Chapman, 'Fixed capital formation', p. 240.
2 *Ibid.*
3 Lee, *M'Connel and Kennedy*, pp. 139–40.
4 *Ibid.*, p. 140.
5 *P.P.* 1833, 'Report from the Select Committee on Manufactures, Commerce and Shipping', p. 45.
6 Crouzet (ed.), *Capital Formation*, pp. 195–6, quotes profit levels approaching 20 per cent before 1815; and Cottrell, *Industrial Finance*, p. 24, shows the fall in profit rates in the second quarter of the nineteenth century.
7 Chapman, 'Fixed capital formation', p. 240.
8 V. A. C. Gatrell, 'Labour, power and the size of firms in Lancashire cotton in the second quarter of the nineteenth century', *Economic History Review*, XXX, 1977, p. 97.
9 The results were published in 1788, in a monograph entitled 'An important crisis in the cotton manufacturing of Great Britain explained'.
10 G. Unwin, *Samuel Oldknow and the Arkwrights. The Industrial Revolution at Stockport and Marple*, Manchester, 1924, p. 115.
11 The recent researches of Gatrell and of Lloyd-Jones and Le Roux indicate the small size of many early mills. Gatrell, 'Lancashire cotton', pp. 95–139; and Lloyd-Jones and Le Roux, 'Size of firms', pp. 72–80.
12 E. Baines, *History of the Cotton Manufacture in Great Britain*, London, 1835, p. 219.
13 Though in fact considerable refinement was necessary. For help in this exercise I am grateful to Dr S. D. Chapman.
14 Outlined in Chapter II.
15 The only exception was J. Parker, a London lawyer.
16 A. P. Wadsworth and J. L. Mann, *The Cotton Trade and Industrial Lancashire 1600–1780*, Manchester, 1931, pp. 288–302.
17 Raffald, *Directory for 1772*.

18   W. Bailey, *Northern Directory*, 1781.

19   S. D. Chapman, 'The Peels in the early English cotton industry', *Business History*, XI, 1969, p. 81.

20   O. Ashmore, 'Low Moor, Clitheroe: a nineteenth century factory community', *Transactions of the Lancashire and Cheshire Antiquarian Society*, LXXIII and LXXIV, 1963–64, pp. 124–5.

21   J. Foster, *Class Struggle and the Industrial Revolution. Early Industrial Capitalism in Three English Towns*, London, 1974, p. 12.

22   Chapman, *Factory Masters*, p. 95; also referred to in Chapter IV.

23   J. Sleigh, 'The old Ashbourne families', *Derbyshire Archaeological Journal*, III, 1881, p. 4.

24   *UBD*, 1, 1790.

25   Fitton and Wadsworth, *Strutts and Arkwrights*, p. 86.

26   J. Lindsay, 'An early industrial community: the Evans cotton mill at Darley Abbey, Derbyshire, 1783–1810', *Business History Review*, XXXIV, 1960, pp. 277–301.

27   P. Mathias, *The Transformation of England*, London, 1979, p. 106.

28   C. Aspin and S. D. Chapman, *James Hargreaves and the Spinning Jenny*, Preston, 1964, chapter I.

29   Bailey, *Directory*, 1783.

30   Mathias, *The Brewing Industry*, p. 323.

31   H. Crump and G. Ghorbal, *History of the Huddersfield Woollen Industry*, Huddersfield, 1935, p. 60.

32   J. Hodgson, *History of Manufacturing and other Industries of Keighley*, Keighley, 1879, pp. 212–13.

33   Fitton and Wadsworth, *Strutts and Arkwrights*, p. 93 n., and mss in Lancashire Record Office, DDPr/62/1: 'Agreement between John Chadwick & Richard Arkwright of Cromford for lease of new spinning mill at Birkacre, 29 November 1777'; and 'Surrender of property after its destruction by "a riotous mob"', 24 September 1780.

34   Hodgson, *Industries of Keighley*, pp. 52 and 217–19.

35   E.g. Miss Rachel Leach, *ibid.*, p. 214; and Joseph Smith, *ibid.*, pp. 222–3.

36   Which was superseded by Peter Atherton & Co. after 1787.

37   E. J. Foulkes, 'The cotton spinning factories of Flintshire 1777–1866', *Flintshire Historical Society Publications*, XXI, 1964, p. 93, and Chapman, *Factory Masters*, p. 74.

38   William Douglas (Raffald, *Directory for 1772*; Bailey, *Directory* 1781); Daniel and John Whitaker (Rafflad 1772, Bailey 1781);

Christopher Smalley (*UBD*, III, p. 285).

39   Foulkes, 'Factories of Flintshire', p. 92.

40   Possibly rather arbitrary, but nevertheless it indicates broad movements.

41   The practice of promoting a trustworthy employee was common among entrepreneurs who had more business than family members.

42   Chapman, 'The Peels', p. 81.

43   Chapman, *Factory Masters*, p. 91.

44   Fitton and Wadsworth, *Strutts and Arkwrights*, p. 81 ff; and J. H. Crabtree, *Richard Arkwright*, London, 1923, *passim*.

45   Aspin and Chapman, *James Hargreaves*, p. 75, appendix 8 (James family tree).

46   *Ibid.*, p. 22.

47   Chapman, *Factory Masters*, p. 22.

48   *Ibid.*, p. 97.

49   Chapman, 'The Peels', p. 73.

50   Foulkes, 'Factories of Flintshire', p. 93.

51   Chapman, 'The Peels', p. 82.

52   G. Ingle, 'A History of R. V. Marriner Ltd. Worsted Spinners, Keighley', unpublished M.Phil. Thesis, University of Leeds, 1974, p. 9.

53   Sleigh, 'Ashbourne families', p. 2.

54   Chapman, *Factory Masters*, p. 91.

55   R. Owen, *The Life of Robert Owen*, vol. I, London, 1851, p. 85.

56   Mathias, *Transformation of England*, p. 102, makes reference to the tragedy of a family without a male heir.

57   Chapman, *Factory Masters*, p. 79.

58   Mrs Hall, *Memoirs of Marshall Hall by his Widow*, London, 1861, pp. 1–4. G. Henson, *History of the Framework Knitters*, 1831, p. 282. Blagg and Wadsworth's *Nottinghamshire Marriage Licences*, vol. I, 1935, p. 50.

59   Chapman, *Factory Masters*, p. 89.

60   Foulkes, 'Factories of Flintshire', p. 92.

61   *UBD*, III, p. 285.

62   Fitton and Wadsworth, *Strutts and Arkwrights*, p. 62.

63   *Ibid.*, p. 63.

64   *Ibid.*, p. 93 n.

65   Owen, *Life*, p. 73.

66   *M.M.*, 28 October 1783.

67   Foulkes, 'Factories of Flintshire', p. 73.

68   *Ibid.*

69   'Returns of cotton and other mills 1803–4: re Health of Apprentices Act 1802', *British Parliamentary Papers*, reprinted Shannon, 1968.

70   W. Tunnicliffe, *Topographical Survey of the Counties of Stafford, Lancaster and Chester*, 1787, p. 66; and *M.M.*, 28 October 1794.

71   Hodgson, *Industries of Keighley*, p. 213.

72   H. Hamilton, *An Economic History of Scotland in the Eighteenth Century*, Oxford, 1963, p. 172.

73   Chapman, 'Fixed capital formation', appendix F, pp. 262–3, Valuation of Scottish Cotton Mills by the Sun Fire Office *c.* 1795.

74   Chapman, 'The Peels', p. 83.

75   *Ibid.*

76   *Ibid.*

77   Crouzet, Chapman, Gatrell, Mathias.

78   Crouzet (ed.), *Capital Formation*, p. 167.

79   Mathias, *Transformation of England*, p. 97.

80   Chapman, 'Fixed capital formation', p. 237.

81   Unwin, *Samuel Oldknow*, p. 27; and B. Hadfield, 'The Carrs silk mills, Stockport', *Manchester School*, V, 1934, pp. 126–8.

82   Chapman, *Factory Masters*, p. 88, and Bailey, *Directory*, 1783.

83   Chapman, 'Fixed capital formation', p. 237.

84   'List of Apprentices etc.', ms in M.C.L. L/5/1/2/1–2; and F. Collier, 'Samuel Gregg and Styal Mill', *Memoirs and Proceedings of the Manchester Literary and Philosophical Society*, LXXXV, 1941–43, pp. 139–57.

85   J. Brown, 'A memoir of Robert Blincoe', *Derbyshire Archaeological Society, Local History Section*, Supplement 10, Duffield, 1966, p. 25.

86   Deanston, New Lanark, Catrine, etc., were all in isolated country districts.

87   Mathias, *Transformation of England*, p. 103.

88   Pollard, 'Fixed capital', in Crouzet (ed.), *Capital Formation*, p. 149.

89   S. D. Chapman, 'Financial restraints on the growth of firms in the cotton industry, 1790–1850', *Economic History Review*, XXXII, 1979, pp. 66–67.

90   Mathias, *Transformation of England*, p. 94.

91   *Ibid.*, p. 93.

92   G. Shutt, 'Wharfedale Water Mills', unpublished M.Phil. thesis, University of Leeds, 1979, p. 133.

93   Chapman, 'Financial restraints', pp. 66–7.

94   J. Schole, 'Foreign Merchants Guide for 1784', ms in M.C.L; and

Bailey, *Directory*, 1783.

95   Schole, 'Foreign Merchants'; and E. Holme, *A Directory for the towns of Manchester and Salford for the year 1788*, Manchester, 1788.

96   That is, men of great wealth at this stage were rare.

VI

The early cotton spinners: (2) 1811

By 1811 the threshhold of entry into Arkwright-type cotton production had risen sufficiently to push the initial fixed capital requirements beyond the reach of the small man, even though credit for working capital had on occasions become marginally easier to obtain. Alternative technology continued to flourish, however, and in Lancashire, where the cotton industry had become concentrated, factories and workshops employing Crompton's mule constituted an important part of the production process. The significance of this in terms of the present study is that fixed capital costs at least could be, and usually were, lower with this type of technology and its associated organisational pattern than with Arkwright's system. Certainly, evidence indicates that units of production were, on average, smaller and scope for gradual expansion and continuity from domestic production greater in those areas utilising the mule than in those employing the water frame. In addition, capital-economising techniques were plentiful, and there were, as a result, opportunities for individuals of limited means to enter the industry even at this late stage.[1] That is to say, the fixed capital requirements were not necessarily prohibitive, though with respect to working capital pressures the problems were similar to those of three decades earlier.

In order to assess the extent to which the man of limited means entered the industry through this alternative channel, the owners of mule-type enterprises were studied. In 1811 Samuel Crompton, with the assistance of several leading cotton manufacturers, carried out a survey to discover the extent of mule spinning in the cotton manufacturing areas. It was intended to support his case for a government grant in recognition of his efforts.[2]

The accuracy of the findings[3] has been questioned, particularly with respect to the inferred importance of the mule compared with the jenny and water frame. This is clearly a weakness in the survey, as Crompton enumerated jenny and water-frame spindles only where they existed in factories also employing mule spindles. The absolute number of mule spindles, however, is generally acknowledged to be correct, except in Scotland, where only an estimated total was given. This is not serious, as the strength of Scotland as a cotton manufacturing region had declined by the time of the survey. What is particularly pertinent for our purposes is that the number of mule spinning enterprises is unlikely to have been underestimated. Not only did Crompton know the area well, but naturally it was in his interest to illustrate the most extensive diffusion of his technique.

He tabulated his results by township; each mule-equipped mill was listed under the name of the owners or locality. Because over 400 factories were so enumerated, involving more than 1,000 individual entrepreneurs, a proportion of these mills was selected on the basis of an area sample. The mills in the contrasting towns of Oldham and Bolton were chosen. It was believed that a reasonable cross-section of enterprises and of entrepreneurs would be obtained by this means. The cotton industry in Oldham, for instance, concentrated upon the production of coarse yarns, with manufacture taking place mainly in small units. Bolton's specialisation was in fine yarns, which were generally produced in larger establishments, though small-scale production was also to be found.

Edwin Butterworth, a nineteenth-century Oldham commentator, states that in the years 1776 to 1778 six small cotton mills were erected in the Oldham township, three of which were moved by horse power and three by water power. Six were also built in surrounding country areas. All were small, however, and it was not until the end of the century that the three principal mills in the chapelry of Oldham employed more than 100 workers each.[4] As late as 1856 Oldham was 'still remarkable above all other places in the cotton manufacturing district for a great number of small concerns'.[5] This feature was also demonstrated in Crompton's survey, which shows, taking the number of mule spindles as an indication of the size of the mill, that the Oldham mills were significantly smaller than those in other areas. The average number of mule spindles in an Oldham mill was 6,000, and the largest recorded number was 11,000, well below the Manchester average.[6]

The group of individuals involved in the manufacture of cotton in Oldham in 1811 were not as socially diverse as might be expected, given the small scale of enterprise. In terms of background the entrepreneurs can be classified into three separate groups; landowners, individuals with coal-mining connections and those previously occupied in the textile trade, typically in hatting, the local pre-cotton specialisation. Among the wealthier individuals were several who had been involved in the activities of more than one of these groups and who dominated the town's industrial ventures. At the end of the eighteenth century most of the 16,000 population was employed by fifty families, among which four predominated. Each of the four were long-established landowning families who also had coal-mining interests and employed a majority of the textile workers.[7] It was these same wealthy families who provided the initiative and capital for the earliest and largest cotton mills.

The Clegg family, one of the small group of large landowners, was responsible early in the eighteenth century for the revival of the local hat trade, which formed the basis of subsequent textile activities in the area.[8] In 1794 William Clegg was the first local mill owner to apply steam power to cotton production;[9] according to the insurance valuations of 1796, the Clegg family were the most extensive cotton spinners in Oldham, their two mills being valued together at £6,000.[10]

Two of the remaining three families, both named Lees, were apparently involved together in many projects. Daniel Lees, of the 'Werneth' Lees family, began cotton spinning during the 1780s, and erected Bankside Mill in Manchester Street around 1791.[11] In 1794 his son John independently owned a cotton mill, also in Oldham, valued at £2,500.[12] The 'Clarksfield' Leeses had yeoman origins which have been traced to 1556 and in 1776 were named as one of the three principal landowners in the Oldham township. The family erected Holt's Mill, a concern of above-average size for the locality, which was insured for £3,500 in 1792.[13] Additionally they were engaged in three of the four mining concerns of the town, one in collaboration with the Werneth Leeses,[14] and two with the Jones family.[15]

In the 1790s, the Jones family, who owned extensive local land and coal interests, bought Fog Lane (or King Street) Mill, which had been valued at £800 in 1788.[16] This small factory they let to several independent cotton spinners, thus participating in a system which was later to gain importance in many parts of Lancashire but particularly in the Oldham area.[17] Subsequently the family became more active in the cotton industry and took possession of Wallshaw Mill,[18] which they operated for many years.

Each of these families followed a common route to entrepreneurship in the cotton industry: through the diversification of traditional family interests. Agricultural pursuits were extended to encompass exploitation of the mineral deposits on their land. Ultimately, cotton-spinning activity emerged from an interest in the local textile trade. As a result of the successful operation of these diverse interests each family had accumulated considerable wealth prior to setting up as cotton producers. Accordingly, the insurance records indicate that they were not only the earliest but also the largest local mill owners; each mill was valued at £2,000 or more.[19]

Although these four families clearly dominated the economic activities of the Oldham district, several other early entrepreneurs in the local cotton industry had similar backgrounds, as indicated by the results presented in Table 6.1. Joseph Rowland, for instance, belonged to a wealthy land-owning family[20] and had a lucrative interest in local coal mining.[21] While retaining his early activity, with the help of his son he built and ran Orleans Mill,[22] one of the smaller Oldham cotton enterprises.[23] Duncuft, whose family had been substantial landowners,[24] provides a similar example. In partnership with Wroe, he formed the smallest firm listed by Crompton in the Oldham area, and the 1,100 mule spindles were probably worked in part of a factory. This enterprise was clearly only a subsidiary interest for Duncuft, who was also a proprietor of Werneth Colliery, in which he was involved until at least 1826.[25]

Among the mill owners of the Lees district, on the outskirts of
Oldham, were Peter Seville, John and James Dronfield and Ralph
Taylor. Seville was of yeoman origin, his family invested heavily in
the local coal mines, and Peter himself had owned a woollen mill
before becoming involved in cotton spinning around 1788. This
enterprise gained strength, and at his death in 1839 Seville left a

Table 6.1   *Occupational backgrounds of the 1811 Oldham cotton spinners*

Occupation/rank	Social class	No. of men
Textile trades		
Hat manufacturer	II	3
Chapman	II	3
Hand-loom weaver	IV	3
Cotton (small)	II	2
Employee (textile)	III	2
Non-textile trades		
Land (large)	I	11
Land (small)	II/III	7
Coal	I	7
Innkeeper	II	3
Flour wholesaler	II	2
Mechanic (employee)	III	1
Shoemaker (employee)	III	1
Machine maker (employee)	III	1
Unknown		6
Total		52

	Social class	%
Percentage of known total	I	39
in each social class	II	43 or 28
	III	11 or 26
	IV	7

fortune of £60,000 to his two sons, who carried on the cotton-spinning business.[26] The Dronfields also were part of a rich land-owning family, and took over the ancient Hopkin Mill in 1792.[27] This mill as well as Seville's was smaller than average for the locality at the time of Crompton's survey, but in both cases subsequent expansion was substantial and sustained.[28] The Taylor family were 'possessed of considerable wealth'.[29] They initially owned Thorpe Clough Mill, one of the first in the area,[30] and subsequently operated Springside Mill.[31]

It is clear from Table 6.1 and the foregoing description that many of the early Oldham entrepreneurs were ideally placed, in terms of capital accumulation and connections, to become cotton spinners, though none of the above was single-minded in this activity. Not only did they have access to capital, they also owned land on which to build a factory, and most had access to coal deposits which could be exploited when the steam engine was adopted for motive power. So far the results of this study concur with the findings of John Foster. 'Of the first 42 cotton mills built in Oldham between 1776 and 1811,' he comments, 'the overwhelming majority were built by men who started out with capital, and most by men with a good deal.'[32]

Among the Oldham cotton spinners in 1811, however, were a collection of individuals with less considerable resources. Radcliffe Cooper was born near Prestwich of small land-owning stock, and married Mary Greave, whose father was a yeoman of the same neighbourhood. With a small amount of capital and the aid of a partner, Cooper became a small-scale machine-maker.[33] He subsequently established a cotton-spinning enterprise with capital borrowed from his father and his wife's family. In the fullness of time Radcliffe's three sons joined him in the firm and together they built up one of the largest enterprises in business at the time of Crompton's survey.[34] Radcliffe's upwardly mobile course, was clearly helped by his choice of marriage partner and by his own family's small accumulation of capital.

Joshua Bailey came from Holmfirth, near Huddersfield, of a small farming family. Attracted by the good prospects for a would-be cotton spinner in Lancashire, he moved to Oldham, the closest major centre to the Yorkshire border, and established a mill on the outskirts of the town. The mill, financed partly by his parents, was enlarged by Bailey and several successive generations of his family.[35] His case provides a rare example of migration of capital to the Oldham area for the purposes of cotton spinning; the Moss brothers, Edward and Elkemiah, who built and worked the larger of the two mills at Waterhead Mill, in Lees, provide another.[36] Before the brothers moved to Oldham their father, Robert Moss, had been engaged in cotton manufacturing in the north of Lancashire.[37] Robert provided the initial capital for the Oldham enterprise which his sons built up successfully.[38]

Among the 1811 Oldham entrepreneurs, therefore, were some who, with a modest amount of capital, commenced manufacturing in a small way and enlarged the scale of enterprise through the practice of retaining profits. This pattern was also followed by many of the wealthier cotton spinners in Oldham, who began tentatively before committing their capital too extensively in an unfamiliar field. The Wareing family, who had been involved in cotton spinning since 1750, was of the former type.[39] John Wareing, born in 1727, was an innkeeper and small landowner in the neighbouring district of Saddleworth before becoming a small-scale cotton spinner in Oldham. His son diversified the family's activities and increased its assets. Initially he established himself as a flour wholesaler in Oldham and bought more land in the 1780s. John's grandson further expanded the family's holding of land, and on this he built a mule spinning mill in 1802 which was successfully extended by the next generation of the family.[40] At the time of Crompton's survey the family owned two mills, one of average size in Oldham[41] and a small one in Lees.

Robert Whitaker and his son John also achieved some upward social mobility from unpromising beginnings. In 1791, with some savings and some borrowed capital, they purchased a small carding mill moved by horse power, which was valued at £700 in 1795.[42] In 1808, having achieved moderate success, Robert bought a larger cotton mill, which he and his sons built up gradually but soundly. It was a comparatively small mill in 1811, but by 1840, with 1,000 employees, it was the most extensive in the area.[43] Daniel Knott had been a hat manufacturer, and he retained this interest after becoming a cotton spinner. His first factory at Milking Green took five years to complete[44] and, though small,[45] was apparently successful, as by 1811 Knott was the owner of an additional, larger mill,[46] in the Bolton district.

Also of modest origins was Thomas Broadoake, who, in 1802, initiated the first purpose-built cotton factory in Waterhead Mill. He was earlier occupied in the textile trade in a subordinate position when he made a lucrative marriage. His bride, Betty Lees, was the daughter of John Lees, a leading cotton manufacturer and one of the wealthiest men in Oldham. As a result Broadoake was not short of capital for establishing his mill, nor lacking in the connections necessary for maintaining his enterprise and furthering his career.[47]

The origins of the capital utilised by the individuals of more humble background were varied, and in some cases difficult to determine. It is clear, however, that men in this group were more likely than those in the other categories to be non-local, and they tended, for the purposes of capital economising, to adopt a local and wealthy partner. Problems associated with this activity are rarely made explicit, but it should be emphasised that only in exceptional cases was it possible for a small man to gain the confidence of an affluent potential investor.

James Gledhill, for instance, was a native of Yorkshire and originally an operative shoemaker. It is not known when he moved to Oldham, nor whether he continued shoemaking there, but it is certain that he established a small cotton spinning enterprise at Mumps shortly before 1805. He was clearly successful, apparently by practising the virtues of self-help: 'by extreme industry and prudence he was enabled in the course of the succeeding five years to erect a cotton mill at Shore, Greenacres Moor, which in 1815, he so materially extended as to render it one of the largest mills in the town'.[48] It was soon after this that Gledhill, having made a moderate fortune, sold out.[49] It is not known whether he thus severed all connection with the cotton industry, but it is significant that longevity, while not universal among any specific group, was a particularly unusual feature of the enterprises of men of humble origin. It is possible that during his years as a shoemaker, Gledhill amassed sufficient capital to establish a small cotton-spinning mill, though it is more likely that he supplemented his own savings with a loan from a sleeping partner. He was able to expand the mill gradually, by absorbing profits, and eventually he was in a position to build a new, larger one, which by 1811, with 6,000 mule spindles, was bigger than average for the Oldham district.

It is almost impossible to determine by what means a 'poor immigrant' successfully persuaded a wealthy local gentleman to finance an unknown enterprise. Investment in banks or in government bonds, though secure, realised a return of, at most, 5 per cent. It is conceivable that for the individual with spare cash at his disposal the anticipation of profit levels approaching 30 per cent of capital was more than adequate recompense for the risk involved.

The success and virtues of James Lees, like those of Gledhill, have been described in the pompous prose of contemporary local commentators. He apparently began his working life as an operative[50] and was believed to be 'a highly enterprising and spirited manufacturer who rendered the concern of which he was the originator, one of the greatest in the district . . . he raised himself from the extremest drudgery of the spinning room to the position of one of the most opulent inhabitants of the township'.[51] Wallshaw Mill, which James Lees established at Mumps, was one of the earliest and largest in the district.[52] In 1795 it was valued at £2,100[53] and employed 100 people. The mill maintained its position and in 1811 was still one of the largest factories in the locality, with 8,000 mule spindles. The source of Lees's capital is a mystery. It is known that he did not have an active partner, but it is possible that a sleeping partner provided some initial capital. Like Gledhill, Lees sold his mill and disappeared soon after Crompton's survey. They thus differed from the Oldham cotton spinners of moderate or wealthy origins who tended, where possible, to keep the mill within the family for several successive generations.

Daniel Jackson, whose Napier Mill[54] was a small enterprise at the time of Crompton's survey, began his career and his upwardly mobile path in the employ of Peter Seville, a local cotton spinner, at Paulden and later at Milking Green. Jackson clearly impressed his employer, who provided a large proportion of the initial fixed capital for Napier Mill, which was reasonably successful and was subsequently taken over by Jackson's son.[55] Thomas Wroe, the son of Isaac Wroe, a poor weaver, became a publican at Hollingsworth, where he later set up a spinning mill in partnership with Duncuft. Wroe was evidently upwardly socially mobile before becoming a cotton manufacturer, and while engaged in the retail trade he was in a position to accumulate some capital and to acquire valuable business expertise.[56] The quantity of capital so obtained, however, was unlikely to have been sufficient to provide the requisite fixed assets of the cotton-spinning enterprise, despite its small scale,[57] and this explains the adoption of the moneyed Duncuft as partner. Because of his extensive coal interests, Duncuft was probably effectively little more than a sleeping partner, and was probably persuaded to finance the enterprise by the expectation of high profits.

Robert Taylor, senior partner of Taylor & Co., and James Taylor, of Taylor's in Lees, also apparently achieved some upward mobility from modest origins to a position of relative prosperity. Little information on their careers is available, though Robert Taylor was described by Butterworth as a native of Bardsley Brow who 'emerged from comparative obscurity to the rank of one of the principal manufacturers of the place, entirely in consequence of his own exertions'.[58] The details of this substantial rise to prominence are unfortunately not given, but it is unlikely that his origins were quite as mean as Butterworth suggests.[59] James Taylor, like his father, worked as a hand-loom weaver before becoming employed by Ralph Taylor, a cotton manufacturer and member of the wealthy Taylor family.[60] Subsequently, having proved himself able and trustworthy, James was offered a partnership in Ralph's enterprise on submission of a nominal capital investment.[61]

The importance of family connections or wealthy partners to those aspiring individuals with little capital is clearly illustrated among the early cotton spinners in Oldham. The careers of both Wroe and James Taylor, and probably of Robert Taylor also, were greatly aided by the acquisition of connections and subsequently partners. Partners adopted solely for the purpose of finding early fixed assets usually fulfilled their function in the short term, whereupon they were released. Provision was usually made for this, with mutual consent, in the partnership agreement. Marriage to a wealthy partner could be instrumental in the success of a man of limited capital, as illustrated by the experience of Radcliffe Cooper and Thomas Broadoake. Intermarriage among well established families, however, was encouraged in order to consolidate assets.

The information in Table 6.1 indicates that most of the Oldham mills operating in 1811 had been established by men of substantial capital, and the foregoing discussion shows that the largest factories were owned by the wealthiest local land-owning and coal-mining families. A significant role, however, was played by several individuals from what has been designated social class II, whose capital accumulation was modest, but adequate, nevertheless, to cover the costs of minimum fixed assets. The scale of enterprise in the Oldham area was significantly smaller than in other parts[62] and this characteristic, together with widespread capital economising techniques, maximised, in principle, the opportunities available to the men of small capital in this area. There were in fact at least eight individuals in this category (classes III and IV) whose concerns were, for obvious reasons, smaller than average and/or were partly financed by a wealthy partner. Nevertheless a substantial degree of upward social mobility is illustrated by the experience of these individuals. They differed from other groups in their largely non-local origins, and more significantly by the fact that their interest was notably short-lived. Their enterprises either ceased production or changed ownership with great frequency, whereas the large mills belonging to well established families were controlled and sustained by successive generations of the family.

Several alternative explanations are possible. It may be that the upwardly mobile individual had less single-minded aims than his financially more stable competitor, in which case a severed connection with cotton spinning did not constitute a failure, but formed part of a longer-term strategy.[63] The real explanation, however, is more likely to be negative. In sociological terms, an inadequate ability to adopt the essentially middle-class virtue of deferred gratification might ultimately deter the humble man, for whom the practice of retaining profits, necessary for success and expansion, was difficult to maintain. The small man's frequent financial dependence upon a local moneyed partner might similarly result in failure. The partner, often 'sleeping' while waiting for a return on his capital, might find the interval excessive and thus make the decision to cut his losses and withdraw his support. It is clear that if a negative view is accepted, then the pressures of working capital requirements, compounded by the virtual absence of short-term profits, provides a complete explanation of the long-term demise of the man without substantial and constant capital backing. Given the capital structure of industrial enterprises at this time, and the nature of credit acquisitions, the struggle and eventual collapse or withdrawal of the small man is hardly surprising.

Early nineteenth-century Bolton contrasted sharply with Oldham in many aspects of its cotton-spinning production. Mills were larger: the average number of mule spindles per mill enumerated in Bolton was 9,500, and several contained over 20,000. In Oldham, by contrast, only three mills exceeded Bolton's average mule spindle count. Oldham was noted for its manufacture of coarse yarns or even spinning from waste, while the Bolton manufacturers prided themselves on the extreme fineness of their yarns. It is also apparent that the pattern which emerged in Oldham of domination of the industry by a group of influential families was not repeated in Bolton. Data provided by local rate books, business records and other local sources suggest that the majority of the 1811 Bolton cotton spinners had accumulated modest amounts of capital in the textile trade prior to setting up on their own.

The largest group consisted of those who had previously been engaged in local textile occupations, mostly as workshop owners or renters (class II). Reflecting Bolton's early concentration on fine yarns, several 1811 entrepreneurs had earlier been involved in the domestic manufacture of muslin, for which conditions in Bolton were eminently suitable, particularly because of appropriate water quality and locally developed technology. The 1780s and 1790s, moreover,

Table 6.2   *Occupational backgrounds of the 1811 Bolton cotton spinners*

Occupation/rank	Social class	No. of men
Textile trades		
Fustian manufacturer	II	15
Muslin manufacturer	II	9
Bleacher	III	7
Chapman	II	3
Weaver	III	2
Quilting manufacturer	II	2
Cotton manufacturer	II	2
Currier	III	1
Hat manufacturer	II	2
Counterpane manufacturer	II	1
Calico printer	I	1
Mercer and draper	II	1
Merchant	I	1
Non-textile trades		
Land	I/II	10
Retailer	II	4
Banker	I	2
Machine maker	II	2
Husbandman	IV	1
Ironmonger	III	1
Wheelwright	III	1
Unknown		8
Total		76

	Social class	%
Percentage of known total	I	21 or 6
in each social class	II	59 or 74
	III	18
	IV	2

were particularly prosperous decades for the muslin weavers, placing them in a good position to accumulate capital and to invest it subsequently in cotton spinning. This suggests that some capital, at least, for the new process of cotton manufacture was acquired or built up by modest individuals and not simply inherited. That is, in some cases upward mobility was apparent before the rise to entrepreneurship, suggesting that opportunities for the small man existed within the domestic system. Also indicated, therefore, is a continuity of leadership, of capital accumulated in a less developed form of the industry, rather than an emergence of a 'new' leadership.

The Makinson brothers, John and Daniel, joined their father William in his successful muslin manufacturing business, where they acquired expertise appropriate to their subsequent activities. On the death of their father in the early 1790s the brothers diversified their interests and became partners in a small-scale cotton-spinning business while continuing to manufacture muslin with a man named Turner.[64] The Bolton rate books illustrate the pattern of gradual capital accumulation to which this family conformed. The total ratable assessment of the Makinsons' property in 1792 was £5, of which £2 15s (£2·75) was the rate payable on a warehouse, the remainder for a workshop. This places the real value of the property in the region of £140.[65] This constituted only a part of their assets, however, and a year later an insurance valuation considered the whole of John Makinson's property to be worth £1,260, 'machinery and utensils' comprising most of this.[66] By 1796 the two brothers owned the upper storey of a factory rated at £16.[67] Subsequent expansion was indicated by the 1806 and 1811 books for Great Bolton, in which the ratable value of the brothers' property, without machinery or stock, was given as £50.[68]

Among the other former muslin manufacturers was John Wood,[69] whose factory had a ratable value of £24 in 1796.[70] He had become a cotton merchant by 1805,[71] and shortly afterwards he, his brother Roger and a third man, Francis Wrigley, formed a partnership for the purpose of spinning cotton. By 1811 they owned a factory containing 6,700 mule spindles, and although it was one of the smaller local concerns[72], it represented a substantial increase in the value of the partners' assets, indicating some upward social mobility. Joseph Pickering, whose partnership with Platt was clearly successful, had also been a muslin manufacturer on a modest scale. His property, in 1796, was rated at £7 10s and £5[73] and he still occupied it as a muslin manufacturer in 1805,[74] suggesting that he transferred his assets to a cotton-spinning enterprise at a late stage.

John Lum was also a small-scale muslin manufacturer who enlarged the sphere of his activities and increased his capital rapidly. His total assets until 1801 comprised one warehouse, rated in 1795 at £1 10s.[75] In 1801 he owned a small factory rated at £25 which he expanded, and by 1811 the ratable value of his extensively enlarged factory had reached £165, the most valuable in the area.[76] It is likely that, because of the extent of the expansion, it had been assisted by external finance, probably from a sleeping partner.

The final example in this category is provided by the Horrocks brothers and differs significantly from the others, particularly in terms of scale of enterprise and technological innovation. At the age of eighteen, John Horrocks, the enterprising second son of a humble Quaker involved in the textile trade, erected a cotton mill in Preston in 1786. There he employed the Horrocks power loom, the invention of a relative. In 1790 young Horrocks adapted his machinery and became a muslin manufacturer.[77] Such was his success that between 1791 and 1802 he built seven additional factories in partnership with his brother Samuel.[78] He died in 1804 (aged thirty-six), leaving a fortune of £150,000 to his sons,[79] who, together with their uncle Samuel, successfully continued the business at Preston, Turton and Bolton, but reverted to cotton production.[80]

More than 20 per cent of subsequently successful Bolton cotton spinners had been local fustian manufacturers. The Ashworth family are well known in this context, and their careers have been comprehensively documented.[81] They were Nonconformists, large farmers and also actively engaged in manufacturing enterprises. The father of John and Edmund, who themselves became cotton spinners, was an organiser of domestic fustian production, once again indicating continuing leadership. He employed some spinners and fustian weavers of Turton as outworkers and was described as a yeoman and chapman. Henry, John and Edmund's uncle, participated in the local development of the cotton industry as a fustian manufacturer, while retaining his agricultural interests.[82] John Ashworth, like many early manufacturers, was involved in a variety of activities, one of which was cotton spinning; until he completed the New Eagley Mill, which was seventeen years under construction,[83] he continued his father's fustian business in partnership with his younger brother, Edmund. John was apparently not short of capital; the initial cost of the mill was £2,000 and he built nine workers' cottages near by.[84] He specialised in the production of fine cotton, but was not toally committed to it. He retained his interest in agriculture and finally he left the mill in the hands of an inefficient manager in whose charge the business declined.[85]

The two Carlile brothers, members of a prominent Bolton family, were well established as fustian manufacturers prior to 1780.[86] They were still engaged in the business in 1787[87] but moved into cotton production over the following five years.[88] They clearly played an instrumental role in Bolton's rise to importance as a cotton manufacturing centre, and were described some years later by a contemporary local commentator as being among the 'fathers of the cotton trade in this district'.[89] As cotton spinners the brothers were enterprising, and they expanded fairly rapidly, indicating that they held substantial capital resources and enjoyed moderate success. They built Bradshawgate Mill, one of the earliest in the town, and after successfully overcoming the financial difficulties caused by the Napoleonic wars common to most cotton manufacturers after 1796[90] they expanded the enterprise in the early years of the nineteenth century. In 1811 the factory and warehouse together were assessed for rates at £145,[91] the mill constituting the second largest in the town in terms of mule spindlage in 1811. With respect to subsequent progress, the 1821 rate books indicate that the brothers were, in that year, still very much in business and were assessed for rates at £160.[92] The experience of this partnership provides an illustration of the interconnections that commonly existed among cotton manufacturing families. The Carliles were connected through marriage to the Bolling family, and, on the death of James Carlile, Thomas Bolling became manager of the mill, remaining so for four years before successfully merging it into his own concern.[93]

The Lord brothers, James, John and Robert, sons of Thomas, a husbandman,[94] had also been fustian manufacturers, with premises at Blackhorse Street and Halliwell, suggesting that the brothers were upwardly mobile before establishing themselves as cotton spinners. James moved into cotton production in 1793,[95] and the Great Bolton rate books illustrate the gradual expansion of his enterprise.[96] James Lord died early in the new century, whereupon John and Robert took over the business with moderate success.[97] Jeremiah Crook began his career in textiles in a small way as a fustian manufacturer, and his brother, Joshua, with whom he formed a cotton-spinning partnership, was a grocer and bread maker until the beginning of the nineteenth century.[98] Jeremiah had clearly been successful in the fustian trade, and to his enlarged workshop and warehouse was added a small factory, valued at £1,000, at the turn of the century.[99] Shortly afterwards his brother joined him, contributing to the partnership the capital accumulated in his retailing business. Though successful, the enterprise remained modest in scale.[100]

Other previous fustian manufacturers included John Thomasson, whose family was intertwined through marriage and business with the Ashworths;[101] Edward Best;[102] Robert Heywood, who had also been a quilting manufacturer before moving into cotton spinning;[103] Nathaniel Bolling;[104] John Salt, of the Salt Pye partnership,[105] and the Jones brothers, Thomas, John and George, who built the New Acres factory at the turn of the century.[106]

Previous activities in other textile trades are represented among the 1811 Bolton cotton spinners. Thomas Hardcastle, for instance, prior to forming a highly successful cotton-spinning partnership with James Ormrod, had been a counterpane manufacture.[107] Christopher Horrocks[108] and Thomas Smith[109] (of Wylde Smith & Co.) had been engaged in the organisation of domestic weaving previous to cotton spinning. Thomas Ainsworth had a variety of interests; in 1781 he was described as a 'chapman',[110] and in 1794 was classified as a merchant.[111] During the 1780s he was also in a calico printing partnership with Parsley Peel,[112] and in the early 1790s he was again involved with Peel in dimity and muslin production.[113] He thus formed a useful group of business connections, and by 1800 had attained a financial position sufficient for subsequent independent activity.

Richard Kershaw had been a chapman in Little Bolton,[114] and the Sudren brothers, George, James and John, with whom Kershaw was in partnership, were local bleachers.[115] Roger Holland maintained his bleaching concern after setting up as a cotton spinner. He had inherited some capital, and acquired more through activities outside the Bolton area.[116] By 1811 he owned the second largest cotton-spinning business in the town.[117] Also represented among the 1811 cotton spinners in Bolton were those previously engaged as quilting manufacturers, mercers and drapers.[118]

Most of the capital and enterprise for the early Bolton cotton industry was recruited locally, though a group of larger manufacturers, Gray, Gregory and Thomas Wingfield, were obviously migrants.[119] The firm of Gray & Son was the most successful of the three, at least in terms of longevity,[120] and although the enterprise was of only modest scale in 1811 there is evidence that warp spinning was carried on in addition to mule spinning.[121] The firm's long-term success was clearly the result of enterprising diversification in products and markets.

Gray's business dealt with a variety of textile firms, both local and distant, and the business was heavily involved in foreign trading, particularly after 1824.[122] It was in the overseas markets, of course, that the greatest gains were to be made, though the risks were commensurately large. The strength and stability of Gray's enterprise is illustrated by its ability to persist in this area.

The majority of Bolton entrepreneurs so far examined, therefore, were hereditary leaders in the sense that they had previously been involved in a less developed stage of the textile industry. Most were former workshop owners (class II) who had built up their assets gradually before moving into the more lucrative cotton industry. This suggests two things: firstly that opportunities for capital accumulation and upward social mobility existed in the period before factory production, and secondly that it was the same, or a similar, group of individuals who took the early opportunities and emerged subsequently as cotton spinners when further opportunities offered. In other words, there was continuity of leadership as well as continuity of chances of social mobility.

An examination of those whose social and occupational background lay outside textile-related trades completes this chapter. In many instances, as in Oldham, individuals in this category tended to join in partnership with another for whom textile manufacture was a hereditary concern. Examples in Bolton include John Platt, who was a self-employed machine maker (class II), a trade relevant to the emergent cotton industry. He was talented, but his capital assets were modest,[123] so his partner, the wealthier Joseph Pickering, himself a former muslin manufacturer, provided most of the starting capital for their cotton-spinning enterprise. George Grimes, who like Platt undoubtedly contributed valuable technical knowledge to his subsequent cotton-spinning partnership, had been occupied as a machine maker.[124] He moved into cotton production with Joseph Grisedale, who had wide experience in the textile trade and as a cabinetmaker and wheelwright.[125] The enterprise created by this partnership, however, was small-scale and short-lived.

The retail trade constituted the basis of the capital accumulation of several Bolton cotton spinners. Francis Wrigley, for instance, had been a butcher,[126] and Joshua Crook was previously a grocer and baker.[127] Joseph Best had been a malt and hop dealer,[128] and kept the Sun Inn in Bradshaw Gate.[129] He was, however, also engaged in small-scale textile manufacture[130] prior to joining his brother Edward, a former fustian manufacturer in a cotton-spinning partnership. Rowland Hall was a victualler,[131] and with his brothers, Richard, a quilting manufacturer, and Thomas, a currier, established a small cotton-spinning enterprise at Quarlton.[132]

James Ormrod was a banker, and remained so after establishing his 'mill of great magnitude'[133] with Thomas Hardcastle, the former counterpane manufacturer and bleacher. Hardcastle himself subsequently joined Ormrod's banking business to form the famous and successful local firm of Hardcastle Cross & Co.[134] Capital was consequently readily available to meet the requirements of the cotton-spinning business and to finance its expansion. By 1811 the firm was by far the largest in Bolton.[135] Likewise, profits from the cotton enterprise not required for its expansion could be diverted into stocks at the bank. The two enterprises, therefore, were mutually reinforcing.

It has become apparent that the accumulation of capital through land ownership was less important to the development of the cotton industry in Bolton than it was in Oldham. Nevertheless, some of the Bolton cotton spinners were holders of land, typically a small area which in most cases was enlarged as and when the industrial enterprise succeeded.[136] This suggests that land ownership was indicative of the high status which success in the entrepreneurial sphere could make possible.

The majority of 1811 Bolton cotton spinners belonged to families established in the textile industry, and had been involved in branches peculiar to the district, particularly fustian and muslin manufacture. A smaller group comprised men who had previously been engaged in a non-textile business and who, typically, joined in partnership with a hereditary leader for the purpose of cotton spinning. The third and smallest category consisted of those individuals with no previous experience of or contacts in the textile trade but who, like similar men in Oldham, ran small-scale enterprises and did not remain long in the business. This phenomenon perhaps reflected inadequate experience in or commitment to the industry; but more probably, as argued earlier, the long-term failure resulted from financial weakness, which the heavy demands of frequently unexpected working capital exposed.

It emerges from the evidence that the occupational and social backgrounds of the 1811 cotton-spinning entrepreneurs were similar to those of the 1787 manufacturers. In 1811, as in 1787, the majority were hereditary leaders, men whose backgrounds were enmeshed in the textile industry and who began their career in an earlier form of the industry, frequently as workshop owners (class II). In 1811, however, this feature was more evident in Bolton than in Oldham. Transition to the larger-scale and more highly mechanised cotton manufacture was almost a natural progression for the hereditary leaders, or at least a reflection of their success in domestic production. A development of this nature indicated limited yet significant upward social mobility, that is, from class II to class I.[137]

In the previous chapter the extent to which capital was transferred from another sphere of the textile trade was noted. The ease with which this took place can be questioned, but there were clearly advantages in possessing experience in domestic or small-scale textile manufacture. Marketing skills were presumably acquired at this earlier stage, likewise useful contacts and some awareness of financial constraints. These advantages were not necessarily open to individuals previously engaged in non-textile occupations, or to those who had become upwardly mobile from a lower level, which may partly explain their short-term interest in cotton spinning.

Men from wealthy land-owning families formed another major group and constituted the majority of the Oldham cotton spinners in 1811. During the early period of industrialisation these individuals tended to channel substantial quantities of capital into activities other than farming. These activities, which included cotton spinning, were more capital-intensive than other outlets had been and were potentially more lucrative. The immediate motive for transferring capital was to secure a larger return on investment than was at the time possible in land; the longer-term aim was either to increase the family holding of land, or to build up a strong industrial enterprise to be passed on to subsequent generations.

Numerically, the smallest category was that containing individuals owning little or no capital who, with the aid of attributes such as industry and perseverance, and usually a moneyed partner, climbed the entrepreneurial ladder and achieved substantial upward social mobility. The majority of men in this group, however, organised small enterprises and were only temporarily successful.

Because the units of production were generally larger and costlier in 1811 than in the 1780s, and more sophisticated mechanisation entailed greater essential initial capital outlay, it is reasonable to assume that better opportunities for the small man had occurred in the earlier period. In practice, however, little difference was observed between the two periods in terms of the role he played. Because of the variety of organisational and technological methods available, some of which provided opportunities for capital economising, the emergence of the small man remained possible until the mid-nineteenth century.[138] Mule spinning, for example, with which this chapter has been concerned, had changed little with respect to mechanisation and capital requirements by 1811, and could still be carried on in small units. Recent evidence indicates that several firms frequently operated within one factory unit.

Gattrell, for example, emphasises the role of the small man as late as the 1840s, when 25 per cent of all Manchester firms were operating with less than 100 employees; and these enterprises, he conjectures, were reasonably flourishing.[139] More recently Lloyd-Jones and Le Roux, while accepting Gattrell's quantitative base, have refined his argument, and suggest that it was the medium-sized firm (150–500 employees) which was the most typical and requires further examination.[140]

It may be concluded that opportunities for small men to enter the industry were very similar in the early stage of Arkwright-type production and in the later stage of mule spinning. It is, however, possible that, whatever the extent of the available opportunities, a similar type of individual rises to meet the challenge. This individual is most likely to possess some capital and to have had some previous experience in an associated occupation; he is least likely to be without capital and from an unrelated trade.[141]

Adding the results of the cotton study to those of lead, it is clear that some aspects of the initial pattern are reinforced and others modified. Members of previous élite groups, notably landowners and merchants, form an important proportion of business leadership, and it has clearly emerged that men of humble origin, though they existed, tended to fail. On the other hand, a significant proportion of the leadership of the cotton industry had been involved in an earlier branch of the textile trade, either as merchants or smaller-scale manufacturers. Members of the latter group had typically accumulated capital and expertise in their previous occupation and were usually successful in their cotton enterprises.

In broad terms the structure of the industrial élite corresponded to earlier élite groups. The majority of the industrial leaders of the late eighteenth and early nineteenth centuries had either mercantile or land-owning interests. It also seems that there was an equivalent degree of activity lower down the social scale. That is, there was a regular movement in and out of the industrial leadership, as there had been previously in mercantile activities, by men of modest and humble background. This continuous movement, however, though important, made very little permanent impression upon the nature and framework of the industrial élite.

Notes

1   Lloyd-Jones and Le Roux, 'Size of firms', pp. 72–80; and Gatrell, 'Lancashire cotton', pp. 95–139. Both articles point to the persistence of the practice, as late as the 1820s and 1830s, of renting factory space, and that commonly several firms operated within one factory unit.

2   G. J. French, *The Life and Times of Samuel Crompton*, reprinted Bath, 1970, p. 147.

3   The findings of this survey in the two areas are presented in Appendix II.

4   E. Butterworth, *Historical Sketches of Oldham*, Oldham, 1856, p. 117.

5   *Ibid.*, p. 118.

6   Crompton mss *Irving Bequest* (B.C.M.L.).

7   Foster, *Class Struggle*, pp. 11–12.

8   *O.C.* 27 October 1878.

9   Butterworth, *Historical Sketches*, p. 125.

10   Insurance valuation, 1796, CS17/663046. Courtesy of S. D. Chapman.

11   Butterworth, *Historical Sketches*, p. 139.

12   Insurance valuation for John Lees's mill in 1794, 5/631053. Courtesy of S. D. Chapman.

13   Foster, *Class Struggle*, p. 275.

14   Papers deposited by N. G. Rees of Oldham – DDRe/6; and miscellaneous papers DDX 614/19 (L.R.O.).

15   DDX 614/16 (L.R.O.).

16   Insurance valuation for Jones Mill, 1788, 358/551953, 27 December 1788. Courtesy of S. D. Chapman.

17 Butterworth, *Historical Sketches*, p. 139.
18 *Ibid.*, p. 125.
19 Again, this illustrates the small extent of the Oldham mills. In principle, therefore, there was scope for the man of limited means to set up in this area.
20 C. Higson, 'Pedigrees', ms OH 148.34, O.P.L., and Foster, *Class Struggle*, p. 26.
21 Foster, *op. cit.*, p. 196.
22 H. Wilde, *Mills and Mill Owners of the last Century*, Oldham, 1934, p. 41.
23 4,000 spindles. See Appendix II for comparative purposes.
24 DDRe/15/1, L.R.O.
25 DDRe/6, L.R.O.
26 C. Higson, 'Cotton Mills of Lees', mss OH 148.21, and Wilde, *Mills and Millowners*, p. 42 and p. 43.
27 Higson, 'Cotton Mills'.
28 *O.C.* 4 August 1934.
29 G. Shaw, mss, O.P.L.
30 Butterworth, *Historical Sketches*, p. 117.
31 Higson, 'Cotton Mills'.
32 Foster, *Class Struggle*, p. 9.
33 Butterworth, *Historical Sketches*, p. 127.
34 Higson, 'Pedigrees', I, p. 55.
35 *Ibid.*, p. 3.
36 Butterworth, *Historical Sketches*, p. 160.
37 Foster, *Class Struggle*, p. 196; insurance valuation for Robert Moss, chapman, vol. 128/171132, 1759.
38 It was small at the time of Crompton's survey but grew subsequently.
39 Butterworth, *Historical Sketches*, p. 115.
40 Foster, *Class Struggle*, p. 12.
41 Known as Coppice Mill; Wilde, *Mills and Millowners*, p. 49.
42 Insurance valuation, 1795, for Robert Whittaker and son John. Courtesy of S. D. Chapman.
43 Butterworth, *Historical Sketches*, p. 146.
44 *Ibid.*, p. 130.
45 2,400 spindles.
46 9,360 spindles.
47 Higson, 'Pedigrees', I, p. 27.
48 Butterworth, *Historical Sketches*, p. 160.

49 Foster, *Class Struggle*, p. 9.
50 J. Foster described him as a Quaker mechanic, *ibid*.
51 Butterworth, *Historical Sketches*, p. 124.
52 *Ibid.*, p. 118; H. Bateson, *A Centenary History of Oldham*, Oldham, 1949, p. 88.
53 Insurance valuation, CS 8/640362. Courtesy of S. D. Chapman.
54 Wilde, *Mills and Millowners*, p. 53.
55 Higson, 'Pedigrees', I, p. 5.
56 Butterworth, *Historical Sketches*, p. 152; though Foster writes that Wroe's previous occupation was flour wholesaler, *Class Struggle*, p. 11.
57 Only 1,100 spindles, the smallest in the survey.
58 Butterworth, *Historical Sketches*, p. 128.
59 Butterworth was primarily a journalist, and tended therefore to exaggerate those aspects of individuals' experience that his readers would be interested to know. The rise to greatness of a humble man was more likely to receive attention than the experience of a more fortunate individual.
60 Shaw mss, f. 199.
61 This practice was followed by the Peel family. See Chapter V.
62 Illustrated clearly by Crompton's survey. The average number of spindles in a Bolton mill, for example was over 9,000, and Manchester over 11,000, while in Oldham it was only 6,000.
63 Such as spending lavishly or moving into an area with greater returns.
64 UBD, II, 1793, p. 332.
65 Calculation based on the contemporary rate of 9d (4p) in the £.
66 Insurance valuation REXXVI /132945. Courtesy of S. D. Chapman.
67 Real value £425; 'Survey and valuation of property in Great Bolton', 1796, mss, B.C.M.L.
68 Real value £1,350, a 1,000 per cent increase from 1792.
69 *UBD*, 1793.
70 Great Bolton Rate Book, 1796.
71 Holden, *Triennial Directory for Bolton*, 1805, Bolton, 1805.
72 See appendix.
73 £200 and £140 for a workshop and warehouse respectively.
74 Holden, *Directory*, 1805.
75 £35.
76 Worth £4,400, with 10,824 spindles.

77   *Dictionary of National Biography*, Oxford, 1917, p. 1269.
78   *The Story of Horrockses*, Preston, 1950, p. 18.
79   J. Clegg, *Annals of Oldham*, Bolton, 1888, p. 68.
80   He was described in Holden, *Directory*, 1805, as a 'cotton manufacturer'.
81   For example, R. Boyson, *The Ashworth Cotton Enterprise*, Oxford, 1970.
82   *Ibid.*, pp. 1–3.
83   (1787–1804) W. Cooke-Taylor, *A Tour of the Manufacturing Districts of Lancashire*, Manchester, 1842, p. 22.
84   This was a common practice, especially among the larger entrepreneurs. See, for example, Gray mss, B.C.M.L.
85   Boyson, *Ashworth Enterprise*, pp. 5–8.
86   French, *Samuel Crompton*, p. 12.
87   W. Tunnicliffe, *A Topographical Survey of the Counties of Stafford, Chester and Lancaster*, 1787.
88   In *UBD*, 1793, William and James were described as 'cotton manufacturers'; and in Holden, *Directory*, 1805, as 'cotton spinners'.
89   P. A. Whittle, *Bolton-le-Moors*, Bolton, 1855, p. 225.
90   The debts of the Carlile brothers are shown in the Heywood Brothers' ledgers, 1795–96, pp. 459–642, Williams & Glyns Bank, St Anns Square, Manchester.
91   Approaching £4,000.
92   Some £4,260.
93   B. T. Barton, *Historical Gleanings of Bolton and District*, vol. I, Bolton, 1881, pp. 177–8.
94   Abstract of Leases, p. 29, Thompson Collection, B.C.M.L.
95   *UBD*, II, 1793.
96   1794 £12 (value £320) for house and warehouse; 1799, £29 15s (£800).
97   In 1811 their concern was of average size for the Bolton area, with 10,000 spindles.
98   *UBD*, II, 1793.
99   Great Bolton Rate Book, 1806.
100 In 1811 it was one of the smaller mills in Bolton, according to Crompton's survey.
101 Boyson, *Ashworth Enterprise*, p. 5; Barton, *Gleanings*, I, p. 198.
102 Land tax returns, 1794; Pigot, 'Survey of Land in Great Bolton', 1827, ms 90, B.C.M.L.
103 W. B. Brown, *Robert Heywood of Bolton 1786–1868*, Wakefield,

1970, pp. 6–8.

104   Barton, *Gleanings*, I, p. 235.

105   Great Bolton Rate Book, 1796; workshop and warehouse worth £600.

106   Barton, *Gleanings*, I, p. 149.

107   Holden, *Directory*, 1805; Whittle, *Bolton-le-Moors*, p. 225; Barton, *Gleanings*, I, p. 195.

108   *UBD*, II, 1793, p. 331.

109   'Survey and valuation of property in Great Bolton', 1796, mss B.C.M.L.

110   Barton, *Gleanings*, I, p. 243.

111   Abstract of Leases, p. 54, Thompson Collection, B.C.M.L.

112   Chapman, 'The Peels', p. 68.

113   *UBD*, II, 1793, p. 332.

114   Abstract of Leases, p. 16, Thompson Collection, B.C.M.L.

115   Holden, *Directory*, 1805.

116   He does not appear in the local directories or rate books till 1811.

117   His property, known locally as the Four Factories, was worth £7,000. Poor Relief Assessment Book, Little Bolton, 1811, ms 370, B.C.M.L.

118   For example, Richard Hall, quilting manufacturer, Day Book, 1795, Gray mss, B.C.M.L., and Otewell Wylde, mercer and draper, Abstract of Leases, p. 75, Thompson Collection, B.C.M.L., and Holden, *Directory*, 1805.

119   First appearance in local records well into the nineteenth century.

120   Day Book, Gray mss; records of overseas trading till 1830.

121   Stock book and balance sheets 1802–18, Gray mss.

122   Account book, Gray mss.

123   Great Bolton Rate Book, 1796; workshop in Deans Gate valued at £120 (rate £4 10s).

124   Holden, *Directory*, 1805.

125   *UBD*, II, 1795, p. 330. Cabinet and wheelmaker. Great Bolton Rate Book, 1796, warehouse and spinning room £26 (approximately £700).

126   *UBD*, II, 1793, p. 332.

127   *Ibid.*

128   *Ibid.*

129   Barton, *Gleanings*, II, p. 404.

130   Rate Books, 1792, workshop and warehouse, £3 12s 6d (approximately £100).

131   *UBD*, II, 1793.
132   3,280 spindles (fourth smallest).
133   Whittle, *Bolton-le-Moors*, pp. 217–18.
134   Barton, *Gleanings*, I, p. 311.
135   39,210 spindles, according to Crompton's survey.
136   Land tax assessments, 1794, QDL mss, L.R.O.; and Pigot, 'Land Survey'.
137   Because of the downward bias discussed in Chapter II, the movement from class II to class I in this case was almost as substantial as a jump from class IV to class II, although it is impossible to measure this exactly.
138   Gatrell, 'Lancashire cotton', p. 97.
139   *Ibid.*
140   *Ibid.*, and Lloyd-Jones and Le Roux, 'Size of firms', p. 73.
141   Hagen, *Social Change*, p. 30.

VII

The lace industry: organisation and finance

The modern lace industry emerged in the second half of the eighteenth century as an offshoot of the hosiery industry. It was geographically concentrated in the Midland counties of Nottinghamshire, Leicestershire and Derbyshire. In the early stages of its development, hosiery machinery was adapted for the manufacture of lace nets. Subsequently a series of attempts to make netted fabrics on hand frames late in the eighteenth century led to the growth of machine-wrought lace production. The emergence of point net in 1768, for example, and Crane's warp net in 1775, resulted from these efforts, and together they formed the basis of a flourishing trade in inexpensive mass-produced goods in and around Nottingham. Previously the city had formed the provincial market for relatively expensive hand-made supplies of lace and net.[1]

Nottingham was an appropriate centre for lace production. Hosiery had been made there for some years, and in the 1760s the earliest units of cotton manufacture were situated in the town.[2] As a result, a suitably skilled work force existed there. The merchants and manufacturers possessed experience and expertise in the textile trade and had formed connections useful for their future development. There were, moreover, long-distance communications to other textile areas, particularly the cotton regions of Lancashire, from where vital raw materials were supplied.

In 1808 Heathcoat's innovation, the bobbin net machine, was patented. Being based on a collection of previously unsuccessful attempts to imitate the pillow net process, the machine was not entirely original, but its repercussions on the local industry were far-reaching. The potential of the bobbin net machine, which copied hand-made lace on a factory scale, was quickly appreciated in the Nottingham area, and 'nearly all the mechanical skill and spare capital of the district'[3] was invested in the new process. Had it not been for the protection of Heathcoat's patent, which, however, was not fully effective, the rush would doubtless have been greater.

It has been observed that lace was one of the first industries to originate during the factory age[4] and that machine-made lace-making was factory-based almost from the start.[5] It is clear, however, that although several lace manufacturers housed steam-powered machines in factory premises the vast majority of entrepreneurs were owners or renters of a small number of machines typically operated in rented accommodation. It was not until the late 1840s and 1850s that purpose-designed factories were constructed on a large scale,[6] by which time the number of capitalists was much reduced.

Because of the patent the immediate impact of Heathcoat's development was subdued, but on its expiry in 1823 great quantities of capital flowed into the industry from 'bankers, lawyers, landowners, farmers, retail dealers . . .'[7] in order to construct and utilise new lace machinery. The availability of capital generated within local industries and the presence of experienced labour and mechanics skilled in the repair and adaptation of knitting frames created an environment advantageous to the development of the local industry and to the emergence of a large new group of entrepreneurs.

It has commonly been assumed by historians of the lace industry that the initial fixed capital requirements were sufficiently small to permit the individual of modest means to become established in the trade. In principle, the early lace industry favoured the small man by remaining essentially small-scale and workshop-based at least until the 1840s.[8] Premises were simple, and facilities for renting them, and the necessary machinery were readily available to all. As a result, parallels have been drawn between the opportunities that existed for upward social mobility in the lace industry of the early nineteenth century, and late eighteenth century cotton manufacture. 'The artisan classes of the hosiery districts', it has been suggested, 'had to wait until the opening of the lace manufacture in the second and third decades of the nineteenth century before they were presented with opportunities of climbing the social ladder comparable with those offered in Lancashire after Hargreaves's technological breakthrough.'[9]

In analysing the complex question of machinery costs, confusion arises, it seems, because machine prices fluctuated greatly from year to year. Before the release from Heathcoat's patent in 1823 his machine was available, strictly speaking, only to patentees and licensees, though many infringements occurred before that date. Consequently it was expensive, and ownership was limited to a small group of wealthy capitalists, together with some skilled mechanics who copied the plans and built their own machines. Because, somewhat unexpectedly, the price did not fall after 1823 – perhaps because speculation was rife during 1824 and early in 1825 – the purchase of a bobbin net machine remained costly. The price of a six-quarter machine was £600 in 1825, for example, and a Levers sold for £60–£70 a quarter.[10] The capital outlay on machinery alone was therefore probably prohibitive to all but the most substantial individuals at this stage, though a buoyant second-hand market developed after the slump of 1826. Nevertheless, from the earliest years of lace manufacture there existed large numbers of small independent machine holders, many of whom evidently owned rather than rented their machines.[11]

In the early nineteenth-century lace industry it was common practice to rent machines or to purchase them on credit by instalments, and capital-economising measures were widely publicised. In 1821 a newspaper advertisement stated that 'a twist machine is now preparing by Mr. Wild, framesmith . . . If required it will be sold in half-shares, and part of the money may remain on security of the machine.'[12] Moreover the return on such a machine during 'good' times, and before the industry became overcrowded, was more than adequate to pay off hire-purchase instalments. 'It was,' apparently, 'no uncommon thing for an artisan to leave his usual calling and betaking himself to a lace frame of which he was part proprietor, realise, by working upon it, 20, 30, nay even 40 shillings per day.'[13]

It is clear, therefore, that there were ways in which the man of small means might surmount the apparently prohibitive initial fixed capital costs. During the 'fever',[14] however, even the expense involved in machine renting was considerable, with prices ranging from £12 10*s* to £20 per quarter per year. Nevertheless even an annual rental of £100–£120 for an average-sized machine of six quarters, when spread over monthly instalments, could be within reach of many, provided market conditions were favourable and returns large and immediately forthcoming.

The high rents of the three-year fever period attracted, among others, many misguided and short-sighted speculators from outside the trade who were ruined by the ensuing slump of 1826. The over-supply of machinery in the Nottingham industry exerted a downward pressure on prices and profits, and over-production led to a rapid reduction in the price of nets and an evaporation of consumer confidence.[15] Subsequently machines were sold at scrap value, and a large number of operatives surged into the manufacturing sector by purchasing the better of the discarded frames at the local machine auctions.[16] In this way machine prices came within the range of the enterprising artisan.[17] The price of a Levers eight-quarter machine, for instance, fell from £700 in the period 1823–26 to £150 in the first six months of 1826; during the same period the cost of circulars dropped from £650 to £130, and that of pushers and travers warps from £480–500 to £80–120.[18] Prices fell still further in the later 1820s and the decline continued. In 1832, when the cost of a Levers machine was £4–£6 per quarter, Felkin stated that 'machines are far less valuable than ever before'.[19]

Many of the small machine holders, who by 1829 were suffering from the effects of over-production within the industry,[20] probably emerged during the slump of 1826 when prices, particularly of machines, fell. Earnings, moreover, had been high during the preceding few years, so conditions were particularly favourable for the rise of the individual of small means to entrepreneurship in the lace industry. Moreover the organisation of the industry was unusual in allowing the persistence of the small master subsequent to the introduction of power machinery and factory production. It has been argued that where the domestic system existed, it was quickly shaken off by the rise of a powerful class of machine-owning artisans,[21] though it was sometime after the establishment of this class that the power factory became widely adopted.

The factory, however, was usually small, and was typically owned or leased by a group of machine holders. This effectively minimised the cost of initial fixed assets, and facilitated at least the appearance, if not the long-term success, of the small or moderate entrepreneur. Contemporary newspaper advertisements provide many examples of factory size. 'To be Let, at low rent, a most convenient house situated on Mansfield Road, with an excellent factory attached to it – will hold 8–10 twelve quarter machines.'[22] 'Factory . . . to be let for £25 per annum. Apply Mr. John Scattergood.'[23] In 1833 there were only four powered lace factories in the Nottingham area,[24] all other 'factories' being large shops of hand machines.[25]

Evidence indicates that the majority of manufacturers who emerged in the advantageous conditions in the 1820s owned one or two machines only, and that even as late as the mid 1830s, when the trend towards production in larger units had gained momentum, 'a large proportion (of manufacturers) had only one machine', which was commonly worked 'within a house but little removed above the degree of a cottage'.[26]

As in other industries, the persistence of the small man in lace was facilitated by means of the partnership system, which spread the capital requirement. Advertisements in the local newspaper in the 1830s indicate the prevalence of this. 'A person wanted who can command £2–300 to be employed in the lace business. The advertiser is a machine holder;'[27] 'Lace shop (to be sold) capable of four wide machines now in the occupation of William Bacon, Joseph James . . . 'A desirable investment for a small capitalist.'[28] 'A person in the lace trade is desirous of taking a partner, one that can command a small capital.'[29]

It is apparent that some single machine owners displayed great resilience through the difficult years of the 1830s, but many others, having underestimated working capital costs, became bankrupt during the periods of trade depression. In common with small men in other industries, they mistakenly invested too much of their modest accumulation of capital in fixed assets, and when heavy stocks caused the finishing houses to reduce or terminate purchases they lacked the requisite liquid capital to pay for labour and materials. In circumstances of this nature credit was virtually impossible to obtain, and there was no choice but to cease production and sell out, usually at a substantial loss. Contemporary sources reveal that between 1831 and 1836 more than 500 owners of between one and three machines either sank to the status of artisan or journeyman or left the trade altogether.[30] This follows the pattern observed in the early cotton industry, where small-scale enterprises tended to be successful only in the short term, reflecting a fundamental instability.

A period of unusually high wages provides the most likely explanation of the artisans' ability to pay the cost of machinery and accommodation, which, before 1826 at least, was high. Because Heathcoat had been careful through the patent specification not to flood the industry with his machines, the price of net remained high, as did the wages of a comparatively small number of skilled twist hands. In the preceding period, moreover, generous wage levels prevailed in the hosiery industry. Before the advent of twist net, fancy framework knitters, many of whom subsequently became lace machine holders, were highly paid.[31] In 1797, for example, a contemporary recorded that although plain knitters seldom earned more than ten shillings or twelve and sixpence per week, the highly skilled often received three or five times as much.[32] There was scope, therefore, for select individuals to accumulate capital.

In the lace industry, before the 'fever', the efficient and skilled workman was able, in particularly favourable circumstances, to earn between £5 and £10 per week. Typically earnings were rather less than this. Although Heathcoat paid his workmen between 30s and 60s per week, most artisans in the trade earned in the region of £1. Even at this wage the provident workman might be able to save, and subsequently 'an unusual combination of circumstances allowed many to become machine owners'.[33]

On the expiration of Heathcoat's patent in 1823, workers' earnings rose rapidly. Incomes of £1 increased to between £2 and £4, while the 1,500 men engaged locally in machine building might earn between £3 and £10 per week according to the degree of skill. The concomitant demise of the hosiery trade is illustrated by the level of earnings of the framework knitters, which rarely rose above 12s.[34] During the 'fever' the wages of skilled workmen were unprecedented: £50 or £60 was paid for instruction in the use of the new machines.[35] Setters-up were also highly paid; the fee for adjusting a six-quarter Levers machine, which could be completed by an expert workman in two weeks, was £20. Journeymen framesmiths earned between £4 and £7 per week.[36]

Felkin captured the excitement and uniqueness of the time. 'All were very highly paid and the profits of the masters were great in proportion. During several years the demand was so great that it could not be supplied; the news of such wonderful wages, independence and jolity spread like wildfire. So that speedily machine smiths, locksmiths, and blacksmiths, together with every watchmaker who had a wandering adventurous spirit within fifty or eighty miles, came together in the garrett workshops, extemporised in every quarter of Nottingham.'[37]

The 'unusual combination' of circumstances which provided the working man with a chance to climb the entrepreneurial ladder was short-lived. During this period the industry rapidly became over-supplied with fixed capital and finished products, as a result of which the value of machinery and output soon dropped substantially. A marked fall in wages, which began in 1826 and continued into the 1830s, signified the end of the era of opportunity for the aspiring small man.

The persistence of a group of independent machine holders into the 1840s was facilitated by the 'stall system'. This practice originated in the 1820s and grew in the 1830s. Local newspaper advertisements illustrated the trend. 'To lace manufacturers etc., extensive buildings, comprising a lace factory and large getting-up rooms – in the occupation of Mr. Lambert and others.'[38] Similarly, 'To lace manufacturers, to be let: 1, 2 or 3 rooms together and separately, situate in the market place,'[39] and 'To let, steam power and standing for lace machines.'[40] The advertisements continued throughout the 1840s and beyond.[41] In the mid-1850s factory tenements for stall holding were constructed by established lace manufacturers and by speculators; as during the 'fever', the system enabled the small manufacturer to establish himself with the minimum of capital and gave him the opportunity to share the cost of overheads.

In 1833, during the early days of stall holding, the Factory Commission obtained illuminating evidence on the operation of the system from John Moss, the foreman with Mr Kendall, who owned one of the four power factories in Nottingham. 'It is the largest factory in Nottingham, where there are power twist machines. We work mostly by power; some few by hand of the smaller sort – the boys are mostly hired and paid by the men. Some are paid by Mr. Kendall. A good workman working regularly will be earning above thirty shillings. He has his boy to pay out of that. The boy will have five or six shillings.'[42]

In the age of large-scale factory production the 'stall system' was an anachronism. By dividing the factory into rentable spaces it enabled the small man to continue by avoiding the heavy capital costs that were beyond the means of most machine holders. Naturally, the owner of the factory, the merchant machine holder, benefited from the practice also, as he was able to share the burden of his overhead costs with a number of small independent makers. In the 1850s several of the larger machine-building firms, suffering from declining sales, began to sell their products on hire-purchase terms and to rent them. The small man was thus presented with fresh opportunities and was once again rescued from an apparently hopeless situation.[43]

Announcements in the local newspapers of bankruptcies and dissolved partnerships indicate the fluctuating fortunes of the industry and those involved in it.[44] Partnerships which had been established early in the 1820s, and particularly after the expiration of Heathcoat's patent in 1823, began to break up, slowly at first,[45] but rapidly after 1826 when trade was depressed. Notices of dissolution of partnerships continued throughout 1826 and well into 1827.[46] There followed a temporary respite until late in 1829, when the large numbers of dissolutions illustrated 'the great crisis in the trade'.[47] Although the notices generally indicated failure, occasionally a dissolved partnership was symptomatic of success or expansion, or of one or more of the partners becoming independent. This clearly applied to Thomas Adams, who broke away from his original business associates and set up on his own at this time.[48]

Bankruptcies followed a similar pattern, and the large number indicated in the press during 1826 shrank from the end of that year until early in 1829, when 'thousands of machines',[49] and other bankrupts' effects, were advertised for sale.[50] The depression in the industry extended into 1830 and 1831,[51] when the failure of many of the 1829 machine holders occurred. 'Machinery, property of Mr. J. Hopkin (bankrupt) for sale.'[52] 'To be sold, lace machinery, property of Francis Dexter (bankrupt).'[53] 'Valuable property to be sold, of Joseph Harris of Beeston, lace manufacturer, bankrupt.'[54] The frequency of bankruptcies suggests that enterprises in the industry were small-scale and highly vulnerable, and that only a slight fluctuation in the trade was required to put a machine holder out of business.[55]

The sale of bankrupts' effects at very low prices, moreover, further encouraged the activities of the small man. It was in circumstances such as these that he mistakenly interpreted the purchase of a machine as a way up the entrepreneurial ladder.

As the structure of an industry varied, so too did the function of the entrepreneur. The hosiery industry, as Charlotte Erickson's study demonstrates, attracted 'local and petty rather than large-scale capitalists';[56] and as the lace industry was related to hosiery, and very similar in terms of technology and organisation, it is possible that a similar type of entrepreneur would emerge.

Although the early machines were very expensive, there were from the start numbers of small and enterprising independent operators.[57] 'This sturdy class of small machine holders thrust aside the clutching maw of the domestic capitalist merchant, and set the new trade on a course of development entirely of its own explanations or possibilities.'[58] The entrepreneur in the lace industry, during the 'golden years' at least, was, apparently a humble man of many talents, fulfilling the several functions of the classical entrepreneur.[59]

It has been stated that 'almost every person became anxious to invest something in bobbin net machinery . . . all classes rushed into the arena of enterprise . . . in fact, almost everyone who could raise money to buy a machine (together with a great many who could not) shared in the general mania'.[60] The majority of these investors were proprietors of only a single machine; 'the owner generally works it himself, and so far partakes of the character of master and journeyman, housed in attics . . .'.[61] The small machine owner possessed a 'stoutly independent outlook' and great 'personal ambition'; this 'small and impracticable race', a commentator wrote in 1860, 'set a pattern which has been characteristic of the fancy lace trade ever since'.[62]

The merchant converters, or 'finishers', or 'manufacturers' as they were known locally, provided the major business initiative in the lace trade. A complete entrepreneur, the merchant converter relied on his ability to sell lace and to interpret and anticipate the market's reaction to changes in fashion, income and tariffs. Some specialised, some established a sales organisation, and some purchased finished goods on behalf of overseas importers. 'The sum of these activities is a complex and ever-changing market mechanism, which, from about 1845 had the advantages of a geographical concentration on Nottingham.'[63]

Two distinct categories or 'types' of entrepreneur emerged in the Nottingham lace industry. The large capitalists, similar in character to the merchant manufacturers in the cotton industry, comprised the numerically smaller group. They owned factory buildings, typically less expensive than those in the cotton industry, containing substantial quantities of bobbin net machines. Brown lace was manufactured in the factory, and outworkers frequently handled the finishing processes. The majority of the larger entrepreneurs had accumulated capital during a period of leadership in the domestically organised hosiery industry.

The second category consisted of the numerous small machine owners, many of whom did not survive the depression of the late 1820s and early 1830s. The majority owned between one and three machines, typically purchased cheaply from a bundle of bankrupts' effects, and some had only a part share in a single machine. The older members of this group were previously employed in the hosiery industry as framework knitters[64] and made the transition to lace-making when the opportunity arose and when wages were particularly enticing. Following a period of careful saving facilitated by the high level of earnings, a machine was purchased either outright or by instalment, and independent manufacturing commenced.

'But where,' Felkin asked, 'did they obtain the one million pounds wherewith to become possessed of 3,300 frames and the additional capital and credit necessary for materials to work them? ... The whole was the result of industry, labour, skill, economy and foresight, exercised for the most part during ten or twelve years. While too many, pressed by the after exigencies of the trade, have returned to their original positions of workers on machines, which they for a time owned, the remainder with their successors have built up the goodly trade edifice that we now behold.'[65] The following chapter examines the accuracy of this statement and considers the social structure of investment in the lace industry of the late 1820s.

Notes

1   D. E. Varley, *A History of the Midland Counties Lace Manufacturers' Association*, Long Eaton, 1959, p. 1.
2   Arkwright's cotton mill built in Nottingham in 1768.
3   Varley, *Lace Association*, p. 5.
4   *Ibid.*
5   H. A. Silverman (ed.), *Studies in Industrial Organisation*, London, 1946, chapter by F. A. Wells, p. 49.
6   In this respect a clear parallel can be drawn with the early stages of development in the cotton industry, where purpose-built units of production did not emerge until well into the nineteenth century, after a period of manufacture in units converted from other uses.
7   S. D. Chapman (ed.), *Felkin's History of the Machine-wrought Hosiery and Lace Manufactures*, Newton Abbot, 1967, p. 331.
8   S. D. Chapman 'William Felkin 1795–1874' unpublished M.A. Thesis, University of Nottingham, 1960, p. 147.
9   Aspin and Chapman, *James Hargreaves*, p. 38.
10   Chapman (ed.), *Felkin's Hosiery and Lace Manufactures*, p. 191.
11   Varley, *Lace Association*, p. 43; though purchase by instalments may upwardly bias the impression of ownership.

12 *N.R.*, 9 February 1821.

13 A. Ure, quoted in G. Dodd, *The Land we Live in*, London, 1854, p. 211.

14 The boom period following the expiration of Heathcoat's patent, 1823–26.

15 Chapman, (ed.), *Felkin's Hosiery and Lace Manufactures*, p. 334.

16 *N.R.*, 11 June 1821; and Chapter VIII contains more detailed references.

17 Perhaps too many; the conditions were freak and clearly temporary.

18 Chapman (ed.), *Felkin's Hosiery and Lace Manufactures*, p. 334.

19 *P.P.*, 1833, Factories Commission, William Felkin's remarks, appendix p. 191.

20 Who signed a petition calling for a reduction in the number of hours and whose origins are examined in Chapter VIII.

21 Varley, *Lace Association*, p. 47.

22 *N.R.*, 10 May 1833.

23 *N.R.*, 25 March 1836.

24 R. A. Church, 'The Social and Economic Development of Nottingham' unpublished Ph.D. thesis, University of Nottingham, 1960, p. 98.

25 Factory Commission, 1833, Felkin's evidence, p. 383.

26 For example, Factory Commission, 1833.

27 *N.R.*, 3 January 1834.

28 *N.R.*, 27 May 1836.

29 *N.R.*, 4 May 1838.

30 Church, 'Development of Nottingham', p. 98.

31 S. D. Chapman, 'Enterprise and innovation in the British hosiery industry 1750–1850', *Textile History*, V, 1974. Also examples in G. Henson, *History of the Framework Knitters*, 1833, pp. 174, 238, 385, 416.

32 Sir F. M. Eden, *The State of the Poor*, 1797, p. 276.

33 Chapman (ed.), *Felkin's Hosiery and Lace Manufactures*, p. 145.

34 J. F. Sutton, *Nottingham Date Book 1750–1850*, Nottingham, 1852, pp. 389–92.

35 Chapman (ed.), *Felkin's Hosiery and Lace Manufactures*, p. 333.

36 Sutton, *Date Book*, p. 366.

37 Chapman (ed.), *Felkin's Hosiery and Lace Manufactures*, p. 285.

38 *N.R.*, 16 November 1832.

39 *N.R.*, 13 May 1836.

40 *N.R.*, 27 October 1837.

41 *N.J.*, 3 August 1855, and 10 August 1855.

42 Factory Commission, 1833, C.I., p. 51.

43 Particularly the very high cost of machines.

44 This evidence is necessarily impressionistic; no aggregate statistics of bankruptcies are available, but from the newspaper evidence a picture can be formed of the instability of the trade, and the broad period during which lace firms collapsed.

45 See, for example, *N.R.*, 14 May 1824, 9 July 1824 (Francis Hallam and William Aulton, bobbin and carriage makers), 29 July 1825, 4 November 1825 (partnership dissolved between H. Sutton, G. Oldham and T. Adams, Newark upon Trent mercers).

46 For example, *N.R.*, 18 August 1826, 25 August 1826, 14 December 1826, 29 December 1826, 26 January 1827, 30 March 1827.

47 September 1829.

48 And subsequently became a substantial and long-term manufacturer.

49 *N.R.*, 6 March 1829.

50 In that year no machines were required for purchase.

51 *N.R.*, 29 January 1830; 26 June 1830; 10 June 1831.

52 *N.R.*, 27 May 1831.

53 *N.R.*, 1 July 1831.

54 *N.R.*, 24 June 1831.

55 Only the large capitalists were in a position to withstand these shocks.

56 Erickson, *British Industrialists*, p. 90.

57 Varley, *Lace Association*, p. 43.

58 *Ibid.*, p. 44.

59 S. D. Chapman, 'William Felkin', p. 154.

60 H. Field, *Nottingham Date Book 1750–1879*, Nottingham, 1880, p. 364.

61 Factory Commission, 1833, C.I., p. 34.

62 Varley, *Lace Association*, p. 46.

63 *Ibid.*, p. 55.

64 See Chapter VIII.

65 Chapman (ed.), *Felkin's Hosiery and Lace Manufactures*, p. 339.

VIII

The small masters of 1829

During the 1829 slump a petition was drawn up supporting a restriction of hours worked by lace machines in an attempt to ameliorate conditions in the industry. The petition, or 'Deed', as it became known, was signed by most of the country's lace manufacturers. The signatories numbered 1,211, or seven-eighths of the contemporary machine holders. Because the document,[1] which exists almost intact, contains not only the names and addresses of those signing but also the number of machines each possessed, it illustrates the typically small scale of enterprises at this time. The majority owned single machines only,[2] sixty-seven worked five or more and, of these, thirteen owned ten or more and only three were in possession of over twenty.[3]

The purpose of this chapter is to examine the origins and, as far as possible, the subsequent progress of the small lace manufacturers in the Nottingham area.[4] The early life and career pattern of the forty larger capitalists who did not sign the petition are considered also. The information was taken from a variety of local sources, including burgess records, apprenticeship registers, Watch and Ward lists, local rate books and directories, and census material.

Burgess records.[5] The burgesses or freemen of Nottingham were those individuals to whom the royal charters were granted. In 1835 they numbered three thousand, or between 20 and 25 per cent of all adult males. Admission to their ranks was carefully controlled, as burgesses enjoyed a number of privileges, including the right to vote in parliamentary elections. In order to attain the status it was necessary for at least one of several conditions to be fulfilled. The eldest son of an existing burgess automatically qualified, as did the second son if he had served an apprenticeship. Alternatively the position could be bought, and the corporation was empowered to confer the status upon any individual it wished by this means. In practice, a man whose vote was required constituted the most likely beneficiary. The position of burgess then was not in itself particularly unusual, but it did at least indicate that a man had a trade or had been taught a skill, which suggested an early advantage in life. The source shows that 269 (or 45 per cent) of the 600 lace manufacturers operating in the town of Nottingham in 1829 were burgesses. These men, who constituted a proportion of burgesses larger than in the population as a whole, had clearly enjoyed favourable beginnings.

Apprenticeship records. The apprenticeship records reveal that 50 per cent of those who signed the 1829 petition had earlier learnt a trade through apprenticeship to a burgess. Typically the contract had been made towards the end of the eighteenth century, on expiry of which the individual practised his trade for at least twenty years before setting up in business independently.[6]

Table 8.1 presents the information obtained from this source by area. In central Nottingham 130 (72 per cent) of the 180 apprentices had been placed with framework knitters, and the majority of the remainder had been provided with a training – in setting up frames or needle-making, for instance – beneficial to a future career in lace manufacture. Sixty per cent of the fathers of framework knitting apprentices were themselves engaged in the trade. No pattern emerged among the remaining 40 per cent, who represented an assortment of occupations.

The results from the lace-making suburbs exhibited a similar pattern. In Radford, for instance, seventeen (or 77 per cent) of known apprentices had been bound to the framework knitting trade, in which eight (36 per cent) of the fathers were engaged. As the table indicates, the other fathers were involved in skilled trades, so that by placing their sons as apprentices to framework knitting, they were not encouraging intergenerational upward occupational or social mobility. In Hyson Green the proportion of the total apprenticed to framework knitters was 76 per cent. Sixty-seven per cent of the fathers in this category were likewise engaged; clear instances of upward mobility or even significant intergenerational changes in occupation directly by means of apprenticeship were rare.

Table 8.1   *Occupations to which the 1829 machine holders had been apprenticed*

1. *Central Nottingham*

(a) *Occupation of apprentice*	*No.*
Framework knitter	130
Framesmith	6
Hosier	5
Lace manufacturer	5
Setter-up of frames	3
Sinkermaker	3
Needlemaker	3
Baker	3
Draper	2
Painter	2
Butcher	2
Miscellaneous, including brickmaker, brewer, furrier	16
Total	180

Occupation of apprentices' fathers

(b) *Occupation of apprentice*	*Occupation of father*	
Framework knitter	Framework knitter	78
	Whitesmith	9
	Carrier	8
	Hosier	7
	Yeoman	2
	Wool sorter	2
	Warehouseman	2
	Gardener	2
	Needlemaker	2
	Hairdresser	2
	Tailor	2
	Farmer	2
	Sawyer	2
	Blacksmith	1

Table 8.1   continued

Occupation/rank		No.
	Apothecary	1
	Brewer	1
	Cordwainer	1
	Whittawyer	1
	Woolcomber	1
	Breeches maker	1
	Ironfounder	1
	Maltster	1
	Woodcutter	1
Framesmith	Framework knitter	3
	Tailor	1
	Victualler	1
	Widow	1
Hosier	Hosier	4
	Wheelwright	1
Lace manufacturer	Lace manufacturer	5
Setter-up of frames	Framesmith	1
	Bookkeeper	1
	Labourer	1
Sinkermaker	Framework knitter	2
	d.k.	1
Needlemaker	Framework knitter	2
	Stone cutter	1
Baker	Victualler	1
	Baker	1
	Widow	1
Draper	Draper	1
	Baker	1
Painter	Framework knitter	1
	Shoemaker	1
Butcher	Butcher	1
	Malster	1

2. *Radford*

(a) *Occupation of apprentice*	No.
Framework knitter	17

Table 8.1   continued

Occupation/rank	No.
Lacemaker	2
Brickmaker and maltster	1
Tailor	1
Needlemaker	1
Total	22

(b) *Occupation of apprentice*	*Occupation of father*	
Framework knitter	Framework knitter	8
	Joiner	2
	Tailor	2
	Farmer	1
	Throwster	1
	Fellmonger	1
	Blacksmith	1
	Breeches maker	1
Lace maker	Lace maker	1
	Bleacher	1
Brickmaker and maltster	Brickmaker and maltster	1
Tailor	Tailor	1
Needlemaker	Needlemaker	1

3. Hyson Green

(a) *Occupation of apprentice*	No.
Framework knitter	25
Framesmith	3
Baker	1
Grocer	1
Breeches maker	1
Hosier	1
Butcher	1
Total	33

(b) *Occupation of apprentice*	*Occupation of father*	
Framework Knitter	Framework knitter	16
	Brewer	1
	Dyer	1

Table 8.1   continued

Occupation/rank		No.
	Sawyer	1
	Breeches maker	1
	Apothecary	1
	Collier	1
	Bricklayer	1
	Needlemaker	1
	Widow	1
Framesmith	Framesmith	1
	Tailor	1
	Yeoman	1
Baker	Joiner	1
Grocer	Victualler	1
Breeches maker	Blacksmith	1
Hosier	Labourer	1
Butcher	Cotton spinner	1

4. Basford

(a) *Occupation of apprentice*	No.
Framework knitter	15
Needlemaker	2
Lace manufacturer	2
Setter-up of frames	2
Carpenter and joiner	1
Chemist and druggist	1
Total	23

(b) *Occupation of apprentice*	*Occupation of father*	
Framework knitter	Framework knitter	9
	Joiner and cabinetmaker	1
	Breeches maker	1
	Cordwainer	1
	Setter-up of frames	1
	Blacksmith	1
	Tailor	1
Needlemaker	Needlemaker	2
Lace manufacturer	Grocer	1

Table 8.1   continued

Occupation/rank		No.
	Blacksmith	1
Setter-up of frames	Victualler	1
	Baker	1
Carpenter and joiner	Carpenter and joiner	1
Chemist and druggist	Bleacher	1

5. Sneinton

(a) *Occupation of apprentice*

	No.
Framework knitter	21
Hosier	3
Tailor	2
Bricklayer	2
Baker	1
Brickmaker	1
Linen draper	1
Stocking needlemaker	1
Framesmith	1
Lace maker	1
Total	34

(b) *Occupation of apprentice*

Occupation of apprentice	Occupation of father	
Framework knitter	Framework knitter	15
	Widow	2
	Hosier	1
	Trimmer	1
	Miller	1
	Wool comber	1
Hosier	Hosier	2
	Framesmith	1
Tailor	Tailor	2
Bricklayer	Bricklayer	1
	Widow	1
Baker	Baker	1
Brickmaker	Framework knitter	1
Linen draper	Grazier	1

Table 8.1   continued

Occupation/rank		No.
Stocking needlemaker	Stocking needlemaker	1
Framesmith	Framesmith	1
Lace maker	Framework knitter	1

In Basford and Sneinton the pattern was maintained. Sixty-five per cent and 62 per cent respectively of those recorded were apprenticed to framework knitters, and most of the remainder were learning trades or acquiring skills allied to, or appropriate for, lace manufacturing. Fifty per cent and 71 per cent respectively of the fathers of the framework knitting apprentices were themselves engaged in the trade, and the remainder were occupied either in the textile trade or in another skilled activity.

The results indicate that three-quarters of the apprentices who subsequently became lace machine holders, if only in the short term, had been bound to the framework knitting trade. The movement from the position of framework knitter to one of small lace manufacturer clearly indicated some upward social mobility. This was particularly true in the 1820s when, in terms of income and status, framework knitting became subordinate, certainly in the Nottingham area, to the lace-related trades. Also significant is the strong element of continuity in the occupation of father and son, indicating, at least in the short term, little or no intergenerational mobility. What in fact emerges is that most framework knitters were apprenticed to their fathers, thereby perpetuating the family trade. Where the son was apprenticed to a different occupation little or no change in status was achieved directly by this means. The apprenticeship system, therefore, was not explicitly or obviously used as a means of facilitating upward mobility.

Watch and Ward lists.[7] The Watch and Ward Act was passed in 1812 in an attempt to quell outbreaks of Luddism in Nottingham and the county. Under the provisions of the Act all males over the age of seventeen and assessed to the poor rate[8] were liable to be engaged as law enforcers when required. Individuals fulfilling these conditions

were enumerated in 1812 and again in 1816, when the Act was
renewed. The extant lists resulting from this procedure provide the
name, age, occupation and address of each qualified man, by area.
The information from this source is presented in Table 8.2.

Table 8.2   *Occupation of the 1829 machine holders, from the Watch and
Ward lists, 1812/16*

Occupation	No.
1. *Central Nottingham*	
Framework knitter	120
Hosier	5
Lace maker/manufacturer	5
Victualler	3
Needlemaker	3
Cordwainer	2
Tailor	2
Grocer	2
Setter-up of frames	2
Labourer	2
Cowkeeper	1
Painter	1
Boatman	1
Joiner	1
Wheelwright	1
Dyer	1
Liquor merchant	1
Throwster	1
Framesmith	1
Smith	1
Importer of wines	1
Warehouseman	1
Pattern maker	1
Currier	1
Sinkermaker	1
Brewer	1
Total	162

Table 8.2   continued

Occupation	No.
2. Radford	
Framework knitter	20
Lace maker	2
Tailor	2
Needlemaker	2
Joiner	2
Currier	1
Maltster	1
Victualler	1
Hosier	1
Turner	1
Blacking maker	1
Total	34
3. Hyson Green	
Framework knitter	25
Joiner	2
Cordwainer	2
Baker	1
Draper	1
Bricklayer	1
Butcher	1
Hatter and hosier	1
Framesmith	1
Total	35
4. Basford	
Framework knitter	16
Joiner	2
Needlemaker	2
Setter-up of frames	2
Labourer	1
Skinner	1
Blacksmith	1
Glazier	1
Total	26

Table 8.2   continued

Occupation	No.
5. *Sneinton*	
Framework knitter	22
Lace maker	3
Victualler	2
Framesmith	1
Tailor	1
Hosier	1
Bricklayer	1
Total	31

Of the 162 central Nottingham machine holders of 1829 located in the 1812/16 Watch and Ward lists,[9] 120 (74 per cent) were classified as framework knitters. This proportion corresponds closely to the results from the apprenticeship records. Thirty-five of the remaining forty-two were engaged in trades allied to, and potentially useful for, a subsequent career in lace manufacturing. Thirty per cent of the 1829 machine holders of the Radford district appeared in the Watch and Ward lists. Of these, twenty (or 59 per cent) were recorded as framework knitters, and with three exceptions the remainder were engaged in trades related to lace manufacturing. Seventy-two per cent (twenty-five) of those Hyson Green machine holders found in the lists were framework knitters; related occupations accounted for the activities of seven of the remaining ten.

In common with those in the other areas the men in Hyson Green were well equipped with skills, information and probably also with contacts for making the subsequent transition to the manufacture of lace. In Sneinton and Basford 71 and 62 per cent respectively of the Watch and Warders who subsequently became lace manufacturers had been framework knitters, and most of the remainder were in allied trades. In the outlying districts of Nottingham, with a smaller sample size, the results were similar.

The evidence from this source substantiates the conclusions drawn from an examination of the apprenticeship records. On the basis of the two sets of data it can be said with some confidence that between 60 and 70 per cent of all the 1829 Nottingham machine holders had been framework knitters, and that a further 15–20 per cent had been engaged in other trades related to lace manufacturing. In other words, there was continuity of personnel engaged in the prevailing textile occupations in Nottingham in successive periods. Because property ownership was a qualification for appointment to the Watch and Ward group, it is clear that those individuals discussed above who subsequently achieved upward social and occupational mobility by becoming lace manufacturers did not begin at the bottom of the ladder, or were already upwardly mobile in 1812/16.

Rate books. Three early Nottingham rate books exist which provide information concerning the early economic condition of those who became lace machine holders during the 1820s. The highway rate book for St Nicholas's parish, 1796,[10] indicates the amount of tax that householders or property owners were required to pay for the maintenance of the local roads. A similar record exists for the larger parish of St Mary's, 1801,[11] which is more complete in terms of names and addresses. The third source is a general rate book for a division of St Mary's parish for 1807.[12]

Sixty-one names were located in the 1801 and 1807 rate books for St Mary's which corresponded to those of the 1829 machine holders. The rate levied at this time was 9d (4p) in the £, so it can be assumed that an individual assessed at £3 owned property to the value of £80. The majority of those 1829 machine holders apparently paying rates in St Mary's parish early in the nineteenth century were assessed at between £1 and £4, that is, they owned property worth between £27 and £107. The notable exceptions included William Crofts, whose property was worth £240, suggesting that he owned, in addition to a house, other property, possibly some cottages and a warehouse. William Heath owned property that included a warehouse, as did I. R. Whirlak. Leonard Elliott, described as a framesmith, was paying £25 rates per year for his 'mill' and £12 for four houses.[13]

Forty-two of the 1829 machine holders were ratepayers in the St Nicholas parish in 1796. The method of assessment differed from St

Mary's; the amount of tax payable was given in shillings and pence, which indicates that the rate was collected at frequent intervals, possibly monthly. The uncertainty, however, raises problems for property valuation. The majority of those assessed were charged between one and three shillings in rates, probably every three or four weeks. Men such as Joseph Coleman and Joseph Collishaw, who paid 8s (40p) were substantial property owners, while the largest contributor, William Lowe, paid 9s 6d (47$\frac{1}{2}$p). On the basis of the crude calculation suggested above, his property was probably worth about £200.[14]

The extent of property ownership illustrated by this source indicates that the 1829 machine holders included in the early rate books were advantageously placed to grasp emerging opportunities such as those in the lace industry in the mid-1820s. Although, in the intervening years, there was scope for enlarging property or the accumulation of capital, the possession of some property at such an early stage clearly limits the degree of social mobility involved in the move to lace manufacturer. Generalisations from this source, however, must be treated cautiously because of the small proportion of men included.

For the purposes of this study incidental information was derived from a variety of sources such as the Nottingham Corporation archives and local newspapers. The former contains information on contemporary local issues, such as an inhabitant's refusal to pay rates due. One of the 1829 manufacturers, Thomas Parker, who owned 'messuages and tenements', was reported to have failed to pay rates totalling £3 15s (£3·75) for the years 1811 and 1812.[15] Another, John Wilson of Barkergate, had failed, in 1813, to pay the requisite £5 poor rate for two years.[16] In a different context Edmund Wright, a hosier and owner of some land, was, in 1811, to receive compensation when the new turnpike between Mansfield turnpike and Mapperley Plains was planned to run through his land.[17] Comparable examples in large numbers in the above source are suggestive of the extent of property ownership among a significant group of the 1829 machine holders. The data are impressionistic by nature, but have value nonetheless. They indicate that the humble origins of many of the 1829 lace manufacturers has probably been exaggerated in the literature.[18]

A survey was conducted of the local newspapers in the 1820s, by which time some of the men in the 1829 sample were extensively engaged in the production of lace. In 1820 Samuel Robinson, for example, advertised for sale a doubling and twisting machine of 126 spindles,[19] and Samuel Harvey notified the sale of a five-quarter double-tier twist machine.[20] Since these machines were valuable, the possession of one at so early a stage in the mechanisation of the industry indicated access to capital, through savings, inheritance or patronage.[21] It is unlikely that an individual in the artisan group would have been in a position to put by enough earnings to acquire a machine at this stage, when, because of the patent restrictions and consequent scarcity value, they were so expensive. After 1823, and increasingly so after the slump of 1826, the purchase of a machine from the savings of a workman became more feasible.

William Wild, a framesmith who later became a lace manufacturer, was busily employed making and selling machines in 1821.[22] It was a lucrative occupation, particularly in the early stages of mechanisation when demand outstripped supply and the diffusion of the appropriate machine-building skills was severely restricted. By this means Wild and other enterprising framesmiths rapidly accumulated sufficient capital to acquire and operate machines of their own.

Press notices concerning the activities of individuals in the sample increased substantially as developments in the lace industry gained momentum after 1823. During the 'fever' period, 1823–26, several of the 1829 machine holders advertised for employees, and this was presumably an indication of early strength. In 1824 Mr Stenson and John Daykin, for instance, required additional lace menders; the former stipulated 100[23], indicating a sizeable concern. In the same year Samuel Hall of Basford sought a few 'good workmen' as fitters-up of machines,[24] a category in considerable demand and an occupation commanding high wages providing potential for subsequent upward mobility. In 1825 William Taylor of Derby Road needed '10 or 12 active young women to wind sewing warp and twist cotton'.[25]

The contemporary newspaper columns clearly illustrate the rapid turnover of both machinery and partnerships during the boom and the period immediately after it. They also reveal the extent of involvement of the 1829 machine holders at this early stage. In 1824, for instance, the partnership between William and Joseph Soars, framesmiths, was dissolved[26] to permit each of them to move independently into lace production. In the same year Francis Hallam and William Aulton, bobbin and carriage makers, severed their business connections and each became a lace manufacturer on his own account.[27] Dissolutions of partnerships, with similarly positive outcomes, involving 1829 machine holders continued well into 1830.

The newspapers, as well as secondary sources such as local journals, provide some information about the pre-lace-making days and the subsequent fortunes of some of the 1829 sample. It was found from the Nottingham rate book, for example, that as early as 1803 James and William Elliott, at that time silk merchants, were county magistrates, indicating local recognition and high social status.[28] Similarly, in 1810 William Wilson, a hosier, was elected alderman.[29]

The technical expertise and innovative activities of some 1829 manufacturers are also illustrated. In 1825 John Syner successfully modified a machine to make 'bullet-holes' in lace;[30] William Sneath in 1831 perfected a technique to produce spots on lace net made by the circular comb machine;[31] and in 1839 James Wright applied the Jacquard apparatus to pushers.[32] Thus some of the 1829 manufacturers were exceptional, and the resilience of all is indicated by their survival through the very difficult years of slump between 1826 and 1829.

In an attempt to ascertain the subsequent fortunes of the individuals in the sample, the local directories of 1834 and 1843, as well as the 1851 census material, were examined. Some interesting features emerged. In 1834, following several years of slump, 63 per cent of the 1829 manufacturers listed in the directory were still engaged in lace production (see Table 8.3), confirming the notion that the individuals chosen for study were reasonably resilient. Of the remainder, 12 per cent had moved to retail occupations and only 6 per cent had returned to framework knitting.[33] By 1843, according to the evidence of the directory for that year (see Table 8.4), only 43 per cent of the 1829 lace manufacturers were still engaged in that capacity, while the proportion of framework knitters had risen to 16 per cent.

Table 8.3   *Occupations of the 1829 machine holders in 1834 (directory)*

Occupation	Social class	No. of men	% of known total
1. *Lace manufacture*			63
Lace maker	I	100	
Lace manufacture	I	25	
Lace dresser	III	3	
Lace warper	III	3	
2. *Framework knitter*	III	12	6
3. *Trades allied to lace and other textile trades*			11
Framesmith	II	6	
Hosier	II	5	
Joiner	II	3	
Needlemaker	II	3	
Turner	II	2	
Machine builder	II	2	
Spring maker	II	1	
Hatter	II	1	
4. *Retailers, traders, etc.*			12
Innkeeper	II	6	
Baker	II	4	
Butcher	II	3	
Shopkeeper	II	3	
Grocer	II	3	
Coal dealer	II	2	
Wine merchant	II	2	
Provisions dealer	II	1	
Draper	II	1	

Table 8.3   continued

Occupation	Social class	No. of men	% of known total
5. *Craftsmen and skilled manual*			6
Tailor	III	4	
Shoemaker	III	3	
Currier	III	2	
Brace maker	III	1	
Brazier	III	1	
Hairdresser	III	1	
6. *Professional and miscellaneous*			3
Attorney	I	2	
Constable	III	2	
Auctioneer	II	1	
Boxer	III	1	
Total		209	101*

* Rounding error.

Table 8.4   *Occupations of the 1829 machine holders in 1843 (directory)*

Occupation	Social class	No. of men	% of known total
1. *Lace manufacture*			46
Lace maker	I	72	
Lace manufacturer	I	55	
Lace warper	III	4	
Lace dealer	II	2	
Lace agent	II	1	
2. *Framework knitter*	III	50	16
3. *Trades allied to lace and other textile trades*			10
Framesmith	II	8	
Joiner	II	5	

Table 8.4 continued

Occupation	Social class	No. of men	% of known total
Needlemaker	II	3	
Hosier	II	3	
Bobbin and carriage maker	II	2	
Hat manufacturer	II	2	
Silk edging manufacturer	II	1	
Sinkermaker	II	1	
Machine builder	II	1	
Iron turner	II	1	
Smith	II	1	
Lock and whitesmith	II	1	
Setter-up of frames	II	1	
Dyer	II	1	
4. *Retailers, traders etc.*			11
Victualler	II	8	
Butcher	II	7	
Grocer	II	5	
Baker	II	5	
Beer seller	II	2	
Coal merchant	II	2	
Glass and china dealer	II	1	
Draper	II	1	
Wine and spirit merchant	II	1	
Fishmonger	II	1	
Shopkeeper	II	1	
5. *Craftsmen and skilled manual*			9
Shoemaker	III	6	
Tailor	III	3	
Brace maker	III	2	
Brazier	III	2	
Maltster	III	2	
Cork cutter	III	1	
Currier	III	1	
Trimmer	III	1	

Table 8.4   continued

Occupation	Social class	No. of men	% of known total
Hairdresser	III	1	
Bookbinder	III	1	
Cabinetmaker	III	1	
Painter	III	1	
Rope manufacturer	III	1	
Bookkeeper	III	1	
Brickmaker	III	1	
6. *Semi-skilled and unskilled manual*			3
Warehouseman	IV	4	
Gardener	IV	2	
Cowkeeper	IV	1	
Coachman	IV	1	
7. *Professional and miscellaneous*			5
Gentleman	I	9	
Farmer	I	2	
Constable	III	1	
Accountant	II	1	
Veterinary surgeon	I	1	
Total		296	100

The census data indicate that by 1851 the 1829 machine holders were engaged in a diversity of occupations; the proportion still functioning as capitalists in the lace industry had fallen to 31 per cent and 14 per cent were occupied in the now rapidly declining framework knitting trade (see Table 8.5). The remainder had moved into other skilled work, often in the lace industry, or into retail trade. The census returns also illustrate that a large-scale migration took place during the 1830s and 1840s from the central districts of Nottingham to the new suburbs, which had developed largely as a result of the lace industry, and to the outlying areas.

Table 8.5   *Occupations of the 1829 machine holders in 1851 (census)*

Occupation	Social class	No. of men	% of known total
1. *Lace manufacture*			31
Lace maker	I	52	
Lace manufacturer	I	25	
Lace warper	III	5	
Lace dresser	III	3	
Lace agent	II	1	
2. *Framework knitter*	III	39	14
3. *Trades allied to lace and other textile trades*			14
Hosier	II	9	
Framesmith	II	5	
Joiner	II	5	
Machine builder	II	4	
Dyer	II	3	
Bleacher	II	2	
Needlemaker	II	2	
Hat manufacturer	II	2	
Watchmaker	II	1	
Cooper	II	1	
Lock and white smith	II	1	
Circular bolt manufacturer	II	1	
Smith	II	1	
Turner	II	1	
4. *Retailers, traders, etc.*			16
Victualler	II	9	
Coal agent	II	5	
Baker	II	5	
Grocer	II	5	
Butcher	II	5	
Beer retailer	II	4	
Shopkeeper	II	3	
Furniture broker	II	2	
Provisions dealer	II	1	

Table 8.5   continued

Occupation	Social class	No. of men	% of known total
Newsagent	II	1	
China and glass dealer	II	1	
Innkeeper	II	1	
Eating house	II	1	
Fishmonger	II	1	
5. *Craftsmen and skilled manual*			12
Shoemaker	III	8	
Tailor	III	5	
Cordwainer	III	2	
Hairdresser	III	2	
Maltster	III	2	
Painter	III	2	
Currier	III	2	
Miller	III	1	
Saddler	III	1	
Bookkeeper	III	1	
Bird stuffer	III	1	
Plumber and glazier	III	1	
Bricklayer	III	1	
Staymaker	III	1	
Brace manufacturer	III	1	
6. *Semi-skilled and unskilled manual*			3
Warehouseman	IV	6	
Cowkeeper	IV	2	
Coachman	IV	1	
7. *Professional and miscellaneous*			10
Gentlemen	I	10	
Highway collector	II	3	
Schoolmaster	II	3	
House proprietor	I	2	
Clerk	II	2	
Solicitor	I	2	

Table 8.5   continued

Occupation	Social class	No. of men	% of known total
Constable	II	2	
Veterinary surgeon	I	1	
Colliery proprietor	I	1	
Accountant	II	1	
Surgeon	I	1	
Total		274	100

Twenty-five per cent of the 1829 Sneinton signatories still lived in the district in 1851, and thirteen (or 63 per cent) of them were occupied in the lace industry. Five (or 23 per cent) had reverted to the position of framework knitter, and three (or 14 per cent) were engaged in a non-textile activity unrelated to their pre-lace manufacturing occupations. Of those who had been machine holders in Radford in 1839, seventeen (29 per cent) were still resident there at the time of the 1851 census. Seven of these had retained their links with the industry and seven had turned to an occupation unrelated to that of their pre-lace days. The majority had experienced some downward mobility in the interim.

Twenty-four (or 35 per cent) of the 1829 Hyson Green manufacturers were still to be found there twenty-two years later. More than half were by then engaged in an unrelated trade, while only eight had retained a direct interest in lace. In the Basford district 50 per cent of the 1829 signatories were traced to the 1851 census. Of these, 62 per cent were still engaged in the lace trade, most as skilled workers; 29 per cent (seven) had transferred to a different occupation. Only two of the twenty-four had become framework knitters.

It would have been surprising to find many of the 1829 machine holders still operating as lace manufacturers in 1851. A boom in the industry between 1823 and 1826, reflected in the high demand for lace, created unprecedented opportunities for the emergence of vast numbers of manufacturers, including those of limited means. Indications of over-production were clear by 1829, hence the petition requesting a reduction in hours worked by lace machines. Conditions continued to worsen, and the small manufacturer was the most vulnerable. During the 1830s many small businesses failed, as indicated by advertisements in the local newspapers.[34] Only the largest firms, with scope for diversification, were able to withstand the inevitable slump.

It was expected, therefore, that by 1851 a change in the occupation of most of the 1829 sample would be found. A large proportion of those 1829 machine holders traced to the 1851 census were still occupied in the lace industry, but by this time they were in a subordinate position, and probably in the employment of one of the few remaining large manufacturers in the district. A return to the original occupation might have been predicted, but in fact this was the case with only a small proportion of the sample, presumably because the previous occupation of most of them, framework knitting, had declined in the interim. As a result the individuals displaced by the changing fortunes of local industries acquired alternative means of livelihood, exhibiting little continuity with their previous employment.

The early experience and career patterns of the second type of entrepreneur provides an interesting area of study. In terms of scale and method of operation these larger and more enduring capitalists had much in common with the cotton spinners of the early years of Arkwright-type production. John Heathcoat was one of the most influential figures in the technological and organisational development of the Midland lace industry. One of Samuel Smiles's heroes, he appreciated early the benefits of self-help and self-education. 'I had originally no property and have risen entirely by my own ingenuity and industry,'[35] he modestly and only partly truthfully claimed. He had a rural upbringing in Duffield, near Derby, where his father was a respectable small farmer of chiefly grazing land. At fourteen, young Heathcoat was apprenticed to William Shepherd of Long Whetton, a framesmith and hosier.[36] Following this basic training he joined Leonard Elliott, a Nottingham framesmith, from whom he acquired the technical expertise that was subsequently to be instrumental in his success.

In 1804 he was able to purchase his employer's business, with the financial aid of William Lockett, a Derby solicitor. The initial loan was £500, but many further sums became necessary, and ultimately £20,000 had apparently been advanced from this source. Lockett, however, was only the first, but clearly the most munificent, in a long series of patrons. Mr Seddon, of Leicester, a 'friend', provided financial support for Heathcoat's technical experiments and refinements during 1807 and 1808. Messrs Boden, Oliver and Cartwright, hosiers of Loughborough, supplied funds for the second patent of Heathcoat's bobbin net machine, and at a later, financially difficult, stage Charles Lacy, a Nottingham point net manufacturer and finisher, stepped in with cash.[37] Although little is known about Heathcoat's persuasive techniques, it should be noted that each of these 'beneficiaries' was handsomely rewarded for his support.[38]

Heathcoat eventually succeeded brilliantly, though it is clear that connections were crucial to his achievement by providing most of the requisite capital. His position was maintained by a succession of first-rate managers, the product of his own intelligent decision-making. He was a talented inventor, and his persistent efforts in the workshop were supplemented by his astute interpretation of market conditions. He realised that the potential demand for bobbin net was enormous, and it was his desire to be the first to manufacture this product by powered machinery.[39] Instinct, perception, determination and good fortune all combined to his advantage.

It is clear that much myth surrounds the life history of these larger manufacturers, and several have been incorrectly cast in the self-help mould. Thomas Herbert, who became a large capitalist, is in this category. He arrived in Nottingham, so the story goes, with sixpence in his pocket, which he tossed into the Trent so that he could truthfully assert later that he started out with nothing. He amassed a useful body of knowledge relating to the capacity of machines for adaptation, and from this information produced original, imaginative goods and built up a reasonably large business. Though thrifty, energetic and industrious, he made the mistake of over-specialising.

His enterprise failed when his unusual products suddenly went out of fashion and his stock and uniquely adapted machines became almost valueless.[40] 'Big' Herbert was one of the first lace factory owners in Nottingham and during the unstable conditions of the 1830s helped to extend the life of the 'small man' by encouraging the practice of stall holding.[41]

William Vickers, born in Mansfield in 1797 apparently in poor circumstances, was set to work at the age of seven. By self-effort he became an educated man, and by the time he reached twenty-one he was partner in the firm of Frearson & Vickers, producing fine-quality lace.[42] It is possible that he attained this position by acquiring technical skills relating to the production of bobbin net that had scarcity value, particularly before the expiration of Heathcoat's patent in 1823.

The humble origins of Richard Birkin, a successful lace manufacturer and four times mayor of Nottingham, have been emphasised in the literature of the period.[43] Born in 1805, the son of a poor Belper calico weaver, he moved to New Basford in 1822, where he learned to work a bobbin net machine. Like all good Smilesean self-made men, he spent his spare time reading, drawing or 'contriving objects of utility'.[44] In 1826, as a result of his apparent drive and initiative, he was offered, and accepted, a partnership with his employer. This profitable connection continued for twenty-one years.

William Cope, of Arnold, once described as a 'poor ragged lad without shoes or schooling',[45] became a leading maker of lace curtains. George Moore, to whose background and experiences Samuel Smiles devoted much attention, had an apparently poor start in life. He began his working career as a town traveller for Fisher Strand & Robinson, and his success in this capacity eventually led to the offer of a partnership.[46]

These biographies suggest that the rapidly expanding lace industry offered new and plentiful opportunities for entrepreneurship to men of humble background, particularly in the 1820s. The extent and employment of these opportunities, however, should not be exaggerated. The men whose activities have been described were exceptional and should be considered as such. Determination and industry might attract the attention of prospective partners or potential benefactors, but only in unusual cases. Capital was required and generally could be obtained only from family or friendship.[47] Connections were thus necessary to provide both the fixed capital, which could be minimised or spread among several partners, and the fluctuating quantities of working capital. Only the very unusual or fortunate small man would be in a position to obtain funds by this means. The individuals cited above apparently did so, but the small number of successes indicates that it was not at all easy or common.

Most of the large capitalists in the lace industry as in the cotton industry had moderate beginnings and many, unlike the small manufacturers, were geographically mobile.[48] Thomas Adams, for instance, was apprenticed to a lace manufacturer and merchant in Newark. In the early 1820s he was employed for a short time by H. Sutton and G. Oldham, mercers, at Newark. Leaving in 1825,[49] he moved to Nottingham, where he set up a lace business towards the end of the boom. His firm has been noted for its size and longevity; in 1858, when the industry was declining locally, it employed 500 people.[50]

James Fisher was born the son of a Cumberland farmer in 1775. As a youth he decided against pursuing his father's occupation, and left home with some money to seek his fortune in trade. He had the advantage of useful contacts, and quickly obtained employment with a London haberdasher, where he was quickly noticed as an active and intelligent traveller.[51] 'He early acquired that knowledge of men and insight into the principles of trade which lay at the foundation of his future success.'[52] During the early months of the boom, after the expiration of Heathcoat's patent, having the advantage of some capital, he invested heavily in buildings and bobbin net machinery at New Radford. To supplement his capital he acquired two partners,[53] who provided crucial financial aid when the pressure of unanticipated working capital requirements was experienced. Fisher expanded and diversified his interests, survived the slumps of the late 1820s, and by 1833 he was one of the four big power lace factory owners in Nottingham.[54]

Also of moderate origins were the Nottingham brothers, Samuel and Jonathan Burton. They were apprenticed to a local framework knitter and subsequently gained employment in that capacity. They soon became highly paid point net hands, and in 1831, with the capital they had accumulated, supplemented by family funds, built a small factory. This was successful, and when the partnership was dissolved in 1837[55] the brothers expanded independently still further. Samuel built a factory in Cavendish Vale in 1839, and Jonathan erected a second larger factory behind the original one,[56] which was later expanded.

Samuel Hall, who developed improved techniques for the finishing of lace, was the son of Robert Hall, an early Arkwright-type cotton spinner.[57] He possessed technical and financial expertise and was rarely short of capital. Henry and William Kirkland, a father-and-son team, were lace manufacturers in Beeston. Henry established the Beeston business in 1819, and William, while maintaining his involvement in the factory, also conducted technical experiments. In 1821, with the assistance of a man named Cooper he completed an invention that moved point bars by wheels in place of treadles.[58]

John and William Lambert began work as fancy framework knitters.[59] They transferred to the lace industry during the boom period by investing inherited capital, and maintained their position during the slumps of the 1820s. Late in the 1830s they began to specialise in lace dressing,[60] at which they achieved great success, and their business was one of the few still operating in the mid-1860s.[61] William Nunn also inherited wealth with which he financed not only one of the earliest and largest lace factories[62] but also John Brown's traverse warp patent.[63]

Although these and other lace manufacturers with moderate beginnings constituted the majority of the larger capitalists, they receive much less attention from commentators of the period than the exceptional individuals of humble origin. There are obvious reasons for this, but the role of the small man in the lace industry should not be exaggerated. The financial problems encountered by the large manufacturers, particularly those stemming from the demand for working capital, corresponded to the difficulties experienced by the early cotton spinners. Acquiring credit was particularly troublesome in the lace industry, whether or not favourable conditions existed. Activity was frenetic, especially in the 1820s; overloading of the market was inevitable, and consequently financial institutions, as well as personal contacts, moved with caution. Some capital and solid connections were thus vital to procure success in the long term. Opportunities for the small man in lace, as in cotton, were restricted to the potentially low level of fixed capital requirements. Barriers clearly existed at subsequent stages.

The following pattern therefore emerges. Among the large lace manufacturers, several apparently originated from humble status and, through hard work and good fortune, achieved success. The humble, together with the very rich, however, formed only a minority group within the total entrepreneurial force. The majority emerged from the 'moderate' category. That is, they had some early advantage in life, inherited useful contacts, and were able to obtain some capital from family sources. They were nevertheless upwardly socially mobile in their move to entrepreneurship.[64] Many were geographically mobile, and some acquired mechanical skills which distinguished them from their peers and increased their chance of success. Considerable scope for technological innovation existed in the early lace industry, and many inventors capitalised on their schemes and became successful entrepreneurs.

Product diversification was vital for survival following the initial expansion of bobbin net making, and those who initiated new techniques and products yet remained flexible, were mostly likely to experience success in the long term. Competition was strong, and although opportunities for entry into the industry may have been plentiful, durability was more difficult to achieve and required unusual personal qualities and sound financial backing. The conditions applied even more forcefully to the small-scale manufacturers. Circumstances were optimal for the emergence of a large number of machine holders in the mid-1820s. A change of circumstances in the late 1820s resulted in widespread failure. Only the exceptional manufacturers withstood the shocks of 1829 and the early 1830s.

Because information about 90 per cent of the 700 machine holders in the sample was found, valid generalisations concerning the backgrounds of the early small lace manufacturers are clearly possible. Sixty-seven per cent of these were originally framework knitters, and the second largest group (23 per cent) comprised those previously employed in allied trades as hosiers, framesmiths and needlemakers, for example. Previous retailers, brewers and tradesmen constituted 8 per cent of the total, whereas $2\frac{1}{2}$ per cent of the sample had been unskilled working men, such as cowkeepers,[65] gardeners and labourers.

Significant variations existed within the category of framework knitter, however, which raises problems for the classification of those so engaged. In many respects, and particularly in terms of esteem, the occupation had low status, but while the plain workers were hard pressed to make ends meet in the period before the 1820s, some sectors, particularly the fancy workers, were highly paid. The latter were in a position to save for the future purchase of, or down payment on, a lace machine, while the former clearly were not. It can be surmised, therefore, that the framework knitters who became machine holders had been previously engaged in the fancy section.

As in other industries at an early stage of mechanisation, techniques for minimising initial capital requirements existed, and these aided the emergence of the small man. Facilities were available for renting machinery or factory space, and machines could be bought through hire-purchase schemes or cheaply from bankrupt's effects. Nevertheless, despite the apparent opportunities, only a tiny proportion of the small manufacturers of 1829 emerged from convincingly humble origins, although the extent of social mobility achieved by the remainder should not be underestimated. They had generally climbed the entrepreneurial ladder from occupations that were connected with, though beneath the status of, lace manufacturing, indicating continuity of leadership,[66] or had diverted capital from retailing businesses into lace machinery and premises. Clearly, all the individuals surveyed were upwardly mobile, but significantly the mobility was often only temporary. This corresponds to the experience of the small entrepreneurs in the other industries studied. In some respects the lace industry in its early stage was too easy to enter; it became overloaded with fixed capital, and credit for working capital requirements was impossible to obtain, which effectively doomed the small man to failure. Many men of modest origins, therefore, made use of the opportunities available in the 1820s, but, not surprisingly, they were unable to sustain the position they attained.

Notes

1 The slightly damaged petition is contained in the archives of Nottingham City Library.

2 605 owned single machines; 224, two machines; 98 three machines; and 58 owned four machines (ascertained from deed).

3 It is possible that those refusing to sign were the larger capitalists, but in any event they constituted only a small proportion of the total.

4 The majority of the signatories operated within this area. Those in business in parts of Derbyshire and Leicestershire distant from Nottingham, as well as the several Devon entrepreneurs, were outside the scope of this study.

5 Information supplied by Freda Wilkins, Archivist at Nottingham City Library, 1976.

6 This calculation is based upon the assumption that the men in this category entered the industry during the 1820s, probably following the slump in prices in 1826.

7 Information supplied by Freda Wilkins.

8 For which property ownership was a precondition.

9 The names and addresses were checked against the 1829 deed, in which addresses are given in varying degrees of detail. In the suburbs and outlying areas, where comparatively few men were involved, the district only was named; within the city, however, the name of the street was given.

10 CA 6011, N.C.L. Archives Department.

11 CA 1507, *ibid.*

12 CA 6012, *ibid.*

13 Worth £665 and £320 respectively.

14 .Certainly more than a house, possibly a workshop also.

15 CA 6573, N.C.L. Archives Department.

16 CA 6586, *ibid.*

17   CA 3988/7, *ibid.*

18   For example, the contemporary William Felkin; in Chapman (ed.), *Felkin's Hosiery and Lace Manufactures, passim.*

19   *N.R.*, 30 June 1820.

20   *N.R.*, 4 August 1820.

21   There are several other examples of machines for sale before the onset of the boom, such as John Leavers (*N.R.*, 15 June 1821); Thomas Warsop (*N.R.*, 6 September 1822); H. Leaver (*N.R.*, 24 January 1823).

22   *N.R.*, 9 February 1821.

23   *N.R.*, 30 April 1824.

24   *N.R.*, 14 May 1824.

25   *N.R.*, 11 March 1825.

26   *N.R.*, 14 May 1824.

27   *N.R.*, 9 July 1824.

28   Field, *Date Book*, p. 262.

29   *Ibid.*, p. 288.

30   Zillah Halls, *Machine-made Lace in Nottingham in the Eighteenth and Nineteenth Centuries*, Nottingham, 1973, p. 24.

31   *Ibid.*, p. 22.

32   *Ibid.*, p. 25.

33   The original occupation of most.

34   More information about this is given in Chapter VII.

35   Chapman (ed.), *Felkin's Hosiery and Lace Manufactures*, pp. 180–2.

36   D. E. Varley, 'John Heathcoat 1783–1861: founder of the machine-made lace industry', *Textile History*, I, 1968, p. 3.

37   *Ibid.*, pp. 15 and 18.

38   Particularly Lacy, whose profit from the association was said to be between £40,000 and £50,000, *ibid.*

39   *Ibid.*, pp. 36–37.

40   R. Mellors, *Old Nottingham Suburbs*, Nottingham, 1914, p. 51.

41   *N.R.*, 11 October 1844.

42   Mellors, *Old Suburbs*, p. 230.

43   R. Mellors, *Men of Nottinghamshire and Nottingham*, Nottingham, 1924, p. 222.

44   *Ibid.*, p. 130.

45   R. Mellors, *In and about Nottinghamshire*, Nottingham, 1908, p. 339.

46   Mellors, *Old Suburbs*, p. 52.

47   Banks participated in industry more extensively at this stage than

previously, but capital raised through personal connections was still the norm.

48 Information from the 1851 census indicates that most of the 1829 machine holders worked in the area in which they had been born. My thesis, table XXII, p. 315.

49 *N.R.*, 4 November 1825.

50 W. Wylie, *Nottingham Hand Book*, Nottingham, 1857, p. 80.

51 Chapman (ed.), *Felkin's Hosiery and Lace Manufactures*, p. 320.

52 *Ibid.*, p. 321.

53 Leavers: *N.R.*, 30 March 1827; and Daker: *P.P.*, 1833, Factories Commission.

54 Chapman (ed.), *Felkin's Hosiery and Lace Manufactures*, p. 276.

55 *N.R.*, 5 July 1837.

56 R. Mellors, *Old Suburbs*, p. 149.

57 Discussed in Chapter V.

58 Chapman (ed.), *Felkin's Hosiery and Lace Manufactures*, p. 293; and R. Mellors, *Local Papers*, Nottingham, 1916, p. 42.

59 Watch and Ward lists, N.C.L. Archives Department.

50 *Directory of Nottingham*, 1843.

61 The brothers helped to finance the building of the Theatre Royal at this time. R. Mellors, *Men of Nottingham*, p. 233.

62 Varley, *Lace Association*, p. 34.

63 *Ibid.*, p. 18.

64 In many respects these men corresponded to the workshop owners, class II in the cotton industry.

65 Although cowkeeper was sometimes synonymous with dairyman, the evidence shows that the examples in this study were employees.

66 Again resembling the experience of the early cotton industry.

IX

Conclusion

It was in 1859 that Samuel Smiles published *Self-Help*, a homily on the qualities of character considered necessary for success in mid-Victorian Britain and particularly in industrial activity. The sales of his book, which reached 20,000 in its first year of publication, indicated the wide appeal of his ideas. His sentiments, however, were not original; for example, as early as 1780 William Hutton had exclaimed, 'every man has his fortune in his own hands'. Thus Smiles was reiterating in popular form what the contemporary public wanted to hear. Industrialisation had produced so many unpleasant consequences for the working man that the notion of a beneficial concomitant was likely to be well received. Smiles's views were extensively believed at the time, and the idea that new opportunities for social mobility emerged late in the eighteenth century has been largely accepted ever since.

It is unnecessary to discuss Smiles and his motives; he is mentioned here because of the attractiveness and subsequent influence of his concept of the self-made man. It is implicit in his writings that the description applied principally to those experiencing upward social mobility from humble origins, and he was presumably intending to convey the impression that the phenomenon was not unusual. The concept also has a much wider application, and in principle it can refer to any individual achieving self-improvement, materially, intellectually or spiritually, however limited his rise. This more extensive definition clearly has greater applicability during the period under study than the former idealistic interpretation.

It is frequently argued that during the early stages of

industrialisation unprecedented opportunities existed for individuals from diverse social origins to attain positions of industrial power.[1] The seizure of such opportunities was facilitated by the interaction of economic and social change and particularly by the growing openness of society.[2] The results of the present study, designed to test the proposition, indicate the type of individual who successfully took advantage of the apparently unusual opportunities that opened up.

Examination of the early sough masters in the lead-mining industry clearly revealed the small amount of capital and enterprise provided by individuals of humble origin. The recruitment of entrepreneurial strength was weighted heavily on the side of high-status land and lead-based occupations. It may be argued that, because the study concentrated on the sough masters, the larger capitalists in the field of lead mining, this result was inevitable. The sough masters, however, were chosen because there existed more opportunities for sustained upward social mobility and long-term industrial leadership from sough driving than from simple lead mining. Moreover the small size of many shares implied that initial capital investment did not have to be prohibitive to the enterprising individual with only modest savings.

In practice, however, probably because investment in the lead mines and soughs was a gamble, and because a lengthy and continuous period of investment was frequently necessary before any return was forthcoming, the role of the small investor was insubstantial and typically short-term. It was the individual with capital or good connections who became the longer-term capitalist. Proceeds from sough driving could be great, but equally they could be negligible or negative. Consequently the richer men, who constituted the majority of sough masters, tended to hold shares in a number of enterprises to increase their chances of success.

The individuals from social categories III and IV and even II could rarely afford to cover their losses in this way, so that unless conditions were unusually favourable investment was forfeited, or such meagre profits made that continued investment could not be justified. Furthermore, gains made early in the life of an enterprise by no means guaranteed a profitable future. Diversification of investment, and thus access to capital, was vital for medium or long-term survival. The unpredictability of most concerns in this field effectively precluded anything but transient industrial leadership for the individual with limited capital.

Table 4.1 indicates that more than 50 per cent of the individuals in the sample had previously been or were simultaneously engaged in land-based occupations. The majority of them were large landowners who perceived investment in soughs as an opportunity to make larger gains than were possible through agriculture, or a means of reinforcing their position of power. A third of the sough masters were earlier or currently involved in activities concerned with the lead trade. Where the proprietors were contemporaneously engaged elsewhere in the lead industry as agents, merchants or smelters, or a combination of these, investment in mines and soughs aided their development in those fields by maintaining a continuous and inexpensive supply of raw material. Some individuals, conversely, became lead merchants or smelters as a result of sough investment. That is, in order to maximise the profits from sough driving, usually received as lead ore, these men established an independent concern. The alternative was to sell their ore, at some loss, to a merchant or smelter. The third important group of investors consisted of local retailers or small businessmen, each intent upon diversifying interest and expanding profit.

Members of class I, therefore, comprised the majority of long-term investors in, and beneficiaries of, the Derbyshire soughs. Individuals from class II were rather less important; those grouped in classes III and IV were neither numerous nor permanent. They were the unfortunate losers: their interest was tentative and of necessity transitory. It is clear that the only individuals who were able to achieve any significant and lasting upward mobility through activities in the lead-mining industry were those who were already fairly wealthy, and who subsequently diversified their interests, usually investing additionally in a more secure enterprise. It is interesting that there are more examples of upward mobility to be found earlier in the period, but once the industry became popular, and abundantly supplied with small investors, opportunities for the small man to attain a position of industrial leadership declined.

The results outlined above are hardly surprising. The amount of capital initially invested by each partner in an enterprise could be, and typically was, small. Subsequent investments in fixed and working capital, however, were often large and unexpected, and exerted increasing pressure before any gains accrued. Credit was virtually impossible to obtain through institutional mechanisms because of the unstable and unpredictable nature of the industry, so informal channels of credit were vital. It was difficult for the small man to form the appropriate contacts and it was more difficult still to persuade these connections, once acquired, to lend capital on such a venture. The risky nature of sough driving, together with the large number of investors involved, reduced each individual's chance of changing his social status either temporarily or permanently by this means. Only the most fortunate of the humble individuals made sizeable gains. Temporary industrial leadership, however, was possible and short-distance mobility a reality.

As lead was a long-established industry, it might be argued that the enterprise of new men could not be expected, and that the conclusions reached by this analysis were the result of sample bias. To check this, a new industry of the period, cotton, was examined. This industry is frequently cited as one offering opportunities to men of diverse origin to attain positions of industrial leadership.

The entrepreneurs in the early cotton industry were examined at two periods: in 1787 and 1811. Table 5.1 shows the results obtained from an examination of all the owners of Arkwright-type mills, according to Colquhoun's national survey of 1787. The majority of these entrepreneurs had previously been engaged in the local textile trade, whose importance was being superseded by the cotton industry late in the eighteenth century. In Lancashire many of the cotton spinners were former fustian or calico manufacturers; early hosiery and silk merchants or manufacturers constituted the majority of entrepreneurs in the Midland counties of Nottinghamshire, Derbyshire and Staffordshire; in Yorkshire former wool and worsted manufacturers predominated. These men, therefore, were hereditary manufacturers, which suggests a continuity of leadership from pre-industrial to industrial production.

In the early phase of the development of the cotton industry there were many techniques to minimise fixed capital requirements. The renting of buildings and machinery was commonplace, as was buying second-hand, and these practices undoubtedly helped the individual with little capital.[3] Despite the opportunities that were available, however, the part played by the narrowly defined 'self-made man' in the early cotton-spinning industry was small. It is clear, however, that a large proportion of the 1787 cotton spinners had emerged from class II with a modest accumulation of capital.[4] They had achieved some self-improvement and therefore fit into the wider definition of the self-made man.

Table 6.1 indicates that the majority of mills operating on Crompton's principle in Oldham in 1811 had been established and subsequently enlarged by men of at least moderate wealth, and the largest and most successful mills were owned by the most affluent local families, who also held extensive land and coal resources. Several former retailers and small textile manufacturers (class II) invested their limited accumulation of capital in cotton spinning, the initial fixed capital requirements for which could still be modest.[5] Although individuals from classes III and IV were fairly well represented among the Oldham entrepreneurs, their enterprises were typically very small, and all were short-lived.

In Bolton in 1811, as Table 6.2 shows, the largest group of entrepreneurs consisted of those who had been engaged in the production of the local textile specialities of muslin and fustian, mostly as owners or renters of workshops (class II). As in 1787, there were few cotton spinners without previous experience in the textile trade, and most of these joined in partnership with another or others for whom textile manufacture was hereditary. This seems to have been a necessary condition for success, as newcomers who attempted to establish a cotton-spinning business independently did not long remain in an entrepreneurial capacity. It is possible that such individuals were not intending to do so, but it is more probable that they possessed an insufficient understanding of the organisation, marketing and finance of the industry, and that their failure was unpremeditated.

Despite the differences between the two periods in terms of technology and organisation, the pattern of entrepreneurial recruitment was remarkably similar. Upward social mobility was present in both periods, indicated by the movement of individuals from class II to class I. There were, however, very few instances of long-distance social mobility, or of new industrial leaders emerging from class III or class IV.

A similar pattern of internal upward social mobility is apparent from the study of the early entrepreneurs in the lace industry. The majority of the 1829 lace manufacturers moved up the entrepreneurial ladder from occupations that were connected with the industry, though substantially beneath the status of lace manufacturer, such as framesmith or framework knitter. Others diverted capital from retailing businesses into lace machinery and premises, by which means they temporarily increased their wealth. On the basis of this information, it can be concluded that most of the individuals comprising the leadership of the lace industry in 1829 had emerged from relatively humble origins, many from class III. Much of this achievement, however, was short-lived, as economic conditions permitting the existence of the small man virtually disappeared during the 1830s. Significantly, the 1851 census returns indicate that most of those 1829 entrepreneurs traced had moved to a subordinate occupation, usually in class III. The opportunities for the small man to attain an entrepreneurial position within the lace industry were clearly exceptional, and, as market conditions changed, most disappeared. Only the very strongest survived.

The lace industry of the 1820s apparently offered the greatest opportunities, at least in the short term, for the emergence of the man of little capital, since 72 per cent of its entrepreneurs were recruited from class III origins. As many as 56 per cent of the 1787 cotton spinners came from class II, mainly as workshop owners, or small textile merchants or manufacturers. Class I individuals from outside the sphere of textiles, such as farmers and businessmen, accounted for a further 38 per cent. Class III and class IV formed the background of only 5 per cent and 2 per cent respectively of the cotton spinners of this time. In Bolton, while the proportion of 1811 cotton spinners from class II was similar to that in 1787, there were fewer recruits from class I and more from classes III and IV. In Oldham, where smaller mills predominated, it is possible that the spinners of class III and IV origins formed as much as 33 per cent of the total, though most of them were successful only in the short term.

The lead-mining industry, certainly with respect to its larger capitalists, apparently offered the fewest opportunities for anything but short-term mobility because of its risky nature and unpredictable returns. Moreover the size and extent of partnerships spread thinly any gains that were obtained. In each industry examined, therefore, there was a paucity of new blood. Leadership was either entrenched because of the traditional nature of the industry, or, in the case of the new industries, it was recruited from a less developed branch of the same industry.

A number of small and modest men apparently made a success of entrepreneurship, at least in the short term, but individuals from the bottom of the scale made little progress. Despite the transformation of the economy and of society *c.* 1750 – *c.* 1830, there appears to have been little real change in the industrial leadership.

It is widely agreed that, because of a variety of economising techniques, fixed capital requirements were unlikely to constitute an insuperable barrier to the determined man of small means. The present study found nothing to contradict this view. The demands of working capital, however, were less predictable, and in the long term usually proved fatal to the survival of the small man. Some writers believe that the man of humble origins with limited local standing and few wealthy connections experienced difficulty in raising the credit necessary for the maintenance of his enterprise. Crouzet refers to the importance of a 'strong local position' to obtain credit,[6] and Mathias concurs. 'They did not need great personal wealth,' he says, 'provided they had a good enough local reputation to command credit and access to a modicum of long-term capital.'[7] Mathias emphasises the value of kinship and friendship links and the personal nature of eighteenth-century society; 'in no set of business relationships were the implications of this more important than in the search for credit'.[8]

Furthermore, these business relationships were typically dominated by middle-class groups which were difficult to infiltrate. As Mathias points out, 'there was a sociological gap between landed, commercial and professional wealth and entrepreneurs in humble stations in life without face-to-face contact'.[9]

There was, however, no intrinsic reason why the small man should have been unable to borrow from such formal financial institutions as did exist. The researches of Anderson and Pressnell show that attorneys and country bankers arranged loans for all social types during the period of industrialisation. The attorney, for example, was 'wont to associate with all manner of people in his search for clients',[10] and customers of the country bankers were drawn from 'all sections of the community'.[11] Cottrell, furthermore, suggests that small men may have been lured into industrial activity by high profits during a boom, and were assisted by banks 'wanting to obtain customers'.[12]

It seems that, far from experiencing difficulty in obtaining loan facilities, the small man might be in danger of becoming too dependent on bank credit at a time when many financial institutions were notoriously unstable. It was thus preferable to be in a position to rely on kinship and friendship groups, not because of the absence of an alternative but because the alternative was unreliable. That contemporaries were cautious of oversubscribing to the activities of banks is clear. Pressnell, for example, has shown the considerable emphasis that was placed upon the extent of bankers' private property. As a bank governor said in 1832, '(i)t is probable that a bank would have no great share of public confidence if the partners of that bank were not supposed to be possessed of large private property'.[13] Moreover, as Pressnell himself says, 'in the eighteenth and nineteenth centuries, the frequent talk of the desirability of demanding security from bankers had some justification in contemporary conditions'.[14]

Individuals who were in a position to arrange private borrowing facilities, therefore, were well advised to do so. The small man, typically having few such personal links, was forced to use the potentially unstable financial institutions where available, and was thus disadvantaged. In times of financial instability, entrepreneurs who relied too heavily on the financial support of the banks might find their business collapsing along with the bank. As Cottrell suggests, 'because of the weakness of many banks, the short-lived industrial firm may have been more typical than hitherto believed'.[15]

It is possible that a change in market conditions partly explains the long-term failure of the inexperienced small or modest man. Excessively low initial capital costs, for instance, may have encouraged the emergence of large numbers of ambitious small men. Many of these would become superfluous as the fruits of their collective labour swamped the market. Only the strongest of those entering the industry under the peculiarly open conditions had a chance of survival.[16]

There is a long tradition of sociological thought and some evidence to support the view that the entrepreneurial role attracts an individual with a particular type of personality, though the possibility remains that a person can adapt to the requirements of the role. D. McClelland's extensive research on achievement motivation, for instance, shows that the individuals most likely to become successful entrepreneurs are those who possess high 'n Achievement' and that there is a strong relationship between this and social class.[17] From his studies McClelland is able to conclude that middle-class individuals typically possess a higher 'n Achievement' than those with an upper-class or lower-class background.[18] According to this proposition men of humble origins are unlikely to become successful or lasting industrial leaders.

It is also possible that small men who achieved entrepreneurial success in the short term may have experienced social or psychological strains in the process of adapting to their new and alien position, thus eventually failing. Acceptance of the small man by better adapted or longer established peers was frequently lacking. Peer solidarity was necessary, not just for moral but also for financial support. Social contacts were important for economic survival,[19] and the formation of these connections could pose problems for the man of humble origins. It is possible, therefore, that economic and social constraints persisted throughout the period of industrialisation which hampered the industrial activity of the small man, while leaving the wealthier entrepreneurs unaffected. Further research may clarify these matters.

The strength of hereditary leadership is less surprising. 'It is no accident,' comments Mathias, 'that much capital for establishing new entrants in an industry came from neighbouring trades or branches of the same trade.'[20] Individuals previously engaged in related industries as workshop owners, merchants, or even those from a subordinate position, had clear advantages over those not so experienced. The former had been in a position to accumulate capital, form useful connections and acquire valuable market information in their early occupation. They may also have developed an appreciation of the potentially heavy demands of working capital, and a sensitivity towards product differentiation or changes in fashion. However determined or enterprising, individuals who had not previously participated in an associated trade and who lacked vital connections would experience some delay in acquiring the necessary knowledge. This study shows that the majority of men, notably in the cotton industry, who attempted to gain positions of industrial leadership from unrelated occupations did so with an experienced partner.

Although it is clear that 'new' men, as well as men of humble origins, experienced difficulties in their efforts to attain a long-term place in the industrial leadership of the country *c.* 1750–*c.* 1830, the explanation is less obvious. A major weakness of a study of this nature is the inevitable bias towards the successful entrepreneur. The background and career pattern of the failed entrepreneur would provide valuable insight into the mechanisms inhibiting success as well as those promoting it. Unfortunately, the unsuccessful entrepreneur, like the failed business, leaves few traces.

The important feature to emerge from this study is the essential similarity between pre-industrial and industrial society in terms of the social origins of those who moved into new openings and those who composed the industrial leadership. In domestically organised industry – as in that organised in large scale factory units – those who became entrepreneurs were either wealthy, often landowners, or men with a moderate amount of capital. This supports Hagen's view that in the early stage of development of many industrial societies the entrepreneurs emerged not from the extreme top or bottom ranks but from a class of moderate men who lacked the high status they desired and perceived entrepreneurship as a means of attaining this.[21] It also corresponds with the conclusions reached by historians of the early modern period, when the extent of mobility into business leadership was clearly similar. Those who moved into the mercantile élite were typically landowners and lesser gentry, and occasionally men of modest wealth.[22]

The range of opportunities open to the small man to reach a position of industrial leadership probably grew from the second half of the eighteenth century, but the restrictions on his mobility apparently remained as insuperable as they had always been. Continuity of leadership was the result. A group of small men were successful in the long term, but they were exceptional and should be recognised as such.

Notes

1   E.g. Mathias, *First Industrial Nation*, pp. 157–8.
2   Perkin, *Modern English Society*, pp. 37 and 225.
3   Capital-economising techniques are described by several authors; see, for example, Mathias, *Transformation of England*, p. 97; Lee, *M'Connel and Kennedy*, p. 15, and Crouzet (ed.), *Capital Formation*, p. 38.
4   Typically acquired during previous activities in the textile trade.
5   Although by this stage initial entry requirements could be very large, enterprises in Oldham were, on average, smaller than elsewhere.
6   Crouzet (ed.), *Capital Formation*, p. 182.
7   Mathias, *Transformation of England*, p. 96.
8   *Ibid.*, p. 101.
9   *Ibid.*, p. 93.
10 B. L. Anderson, 'The attorney and the early capital market in Lancashire', in Crouzet (ed.), *Capital Formation*, p. 246.
11 L. S. Pressnell, *Country Banking in the Industrial Revolution*, Oxford, 1956, p. 246.
12 Cottrell, *Industrial Finance*, p. 35.
13 Quoted in Pressnell, *Country Banking*, p. 235.
14 *Ibid.*, p. 237.

15   Cottrell, *Industrial Finance*, p. 35.

16   This was clearly the case in the lace industry in the 1820s and 1830s.

17   D. C. McClelland, *The Achieving Society*, New York, 1961, p. 256.

18   Studies in the United States show that 50–80 per cent (depending on the definition of categories) of the business elite in the last 150 years has come from middle to upper-class status. Moreover, entrepreneurs tend to come from more diverse origins as development proceeds. McClelland, *Achieving Society*, pp. 276–7.

19   Particularly with respect to raising capital and credit. Mathias, *Transformation of England*, p. 93.

20   *Ibid.*, p. 103.

21   Hagen, *Social Change*, p. 30.

22   E.g. R. Grassby, 'The personal wealth of the business community in Seventeenth-century England', *Economic History Review*, XXIII, 1970; R. G. Lang, 'Social origins and social aspirations of Jacobean London merchants', *Economic History Review*, XXVII, 1974.

APPENDIX I

Examples of 'large' and 'small' shareholders in soughs

Major shareholders (i.e. holders of large shares in one or more soughs; some had interests in other soughs for which the size of holding is unknown).

1. *Richard Bagshaw*
   Magclough 1/4, 1/16
   Brookhead 1/3
   Myners Engine 1/4
   Little Pasture 1/12
   Ladywash 1/8
   Middleton Engine 1/8
   Hounders and Barkers 1/4
   Milnes Engine 1/8
   Moorwood Engine 1/16
   Wheal 1/8
   Bradshaw and Butlers 1/24, 1/48
   Plus small shares in Have-at-all, Haycliffe
2. *J. and A. Barker*
   Stoke 1/6, 1/24, 1/96, 1/768
   Whalf 9/48
   Sellers 5/24
   Blythe 5/24
   Bristhill 8/24
   Black 4/24
   Plus small shares in Eyam Dale, Calver Mill, Wrath, Wheal, Shining Stone, Shining
3. *Barker and Wilkinson*
   Calver 8/24
   Breachside 2/24

Whalf 7/24
Calver 3/24
Cowclose 5/24
Northcliffe 6/24, 1/48, 1/192
Plus small shares in Calver Mill, Shining Stone, Wrathe, Wheal

4. *John Arthurs*
Myners Engine 1/6
Plus smaller shares in Stoke, Milnes & Middleton, Moorwoods, Old and New Bradshaws

5. *Benjamin Ashton*
Brookhead 1/4, 1/24
Plus smaller shares in other Eyam Great Vein soughs

6. *Thomas Gell*
Wheal 1/12

7. *Sir Archibald Grant*
Miners Engine 1/12
Plus smaller shares in Stoke, Milnes and Middleton, Moorwoods, Old and New Bradshaws

8. *Milnes*
Wrathe 11/24
Old and New Bradshaws 1/24, 1/48

9. *William Longsden*
Broomhill 8/24
Little Brookhead 1/16
Stoke 1/6, 1/96, 1/192
Black 3/24
Breachside 2/24
Myners Engine 1/12

10. *Robert Middleton*
Have-at-all 1/12
Ladywash 1/16

11. *William Cooper*
Haycliffe 1/8

12. *Joseph Storrs*
Breachside 2/24 (1765), 12/24 (1806)

13. *Robert Clay*
Eyam Dale Sough 8/24

14. *Nathaniel Staley*
Wrathe 5/24

15. *Charles Potts*

    Have-at-all 1/12
16. *Francis Morten*
    Have-at-all 1/12
17. *Jn. Wilkinson*
    Old and New Bradshaws 1/6, 1/24, 1/48
    Little Brookhead (1796) 1/4
    Calver 3/24
18. *Jn. Twigg*
    Stoke 1/3

Small investors   (none of these also appears as 'large' investor)

1. *Robert Clay*
   Old and New Bradshaws 1/384, 1/768
   Myners Engine 1/48
   Middleton Engine 1/96
   Milnes Engine 1/96
2. *John Cartledge*
   Magclough 1/96
3. *Charles Roe*
   Magclough 1/48
   Myners Engine 1/48
   Middleton Engine 1/96
   Milnes Engine 1/96
   Moorwood Engine 1/192
4. *Hambleton*
   Brookhead 1/96
5. *Wortley*
   Brookhead 1/96
6. *Gell*
   Brookhead 1/48
   Whalf 1/24
7. *Wild*
   Brookhead 1/48
8. *Gascoigne*
   Brookhead 1/48
9. *Mower*
   Myners Engine 1/48
   Middleton Engine 1/96
   Milnes Engine 1/96

10. *Walthall*
    Myners Engine 1/48
    Middleton Engine 1/96
    Hounders and Barkers 1/48
    Milnes Engine 1/96
    Moorwood Engine 1/192
11. *Tipping*
    Myners Engine 1/48
    Middleton Engine 1/96
    Hounders and Barkers 1/48
    Milnes Engine 1/96
    Moorwood Engine 1/192
12. *Isaac Nodder*
    Stoke 1/192, 1/768
    Ladywash 1/96
    Miners Engine 1/32
    Milnes and Middleton 1/64
    Moorwoods 1/128
    Old and New Bradshaws 1/128
    Little Pasture 1/96
13. *Jn. Nodder* (as Isaac Nodder above)
14. *Wagstaff*
    Little Pasture 1/96
15. *Hallow*
    Little Pasture 1/96
16. *Wright*
    Little Pasture 1/96
17. *William Bagshaw*
    Haycliffe 1/128
18. *Robert Bagshaw*
    Haycliffe 1/64
19. *Soresby*
    Ladywash 1/96
20. *Millors*
    Ladywash 1/96
21. *John Watts*
    Ladywash 1/96
22. *Capt. Carleil*
    Stoke 1/96, 1/192
23. *Frost*

Wheal 1/48
Breachside 1/72
24. *Rushton*
Whalf 1/24
25. *Willerson*
Whalf 1/24
26. *Norman*
Whalf 1/24
27. *Robert Scholler*
Sellers 1/24
28. *Wheldon*
Blythe 1/48
29. *Watson and Gilbert*
Blythe 1/24
30. *R. and J. Nollis*
Blythe 1/24
31. *S. Mudden*
Blythe 1/24
32. *Groves*
Blythe 1/24
33. *Thorpe*
Pristhill 1/24
34. Birds
Pristhill 1/24
35. *Buxton*
Pristhill 1/24
36. *Parker*
Breachside 1/72
37. *Fletcher*
Breachside 1/72
38. *Francis Melland*
Shining Stone 1/48
39. *William Mettan*
Calver Mill Sough 1/96
40. *Francis Mason*
Calver Mill Sough 1/96
41. *John Nall*
Eyam Dale Sough 1/96
42. *Stephen Gamble*
Eyam Dale Sough 1/96

43. *Thomas Wingfield*
    Eyam Dale Sough 1/96
44. *Mrs Dowker*
    Calver Sough 1/48
45 *Paul Smith*
    Calver Sough 1/48

Barker and Wilkinson's shares in mines and soughs in 1762

Loss   Wilds Old Grove 2/24
         Brunds Croft 4/24
         Shineing Stone Sough 1/24
         Alderman Mine 2/24, 1/96
         Calver Mill Sough 1/24, 1/48
         Wrathe Sough 2/24
         Wheale Sough 1/24, 1/192
         Have-at-all 2/24
         Northcliffe Sough 1/24
         Misty Know 3/24
         Eyam Dale Sough 1/24, 1/96
         Molsey Meer Mine and Sough 1/48, 1/288
         Busks 3/24, 1/48
         Cresswells 3/24
         Flints 3/24
         Grey Mare 1/24
         Jadloone 1/48
         Long looked for 3/24
         Northcliffe 6/24, 1/48, 1/192
         Nightingales Leas 1/48, 1/96
         Pingles 2/24
         Ratchwood 1/128
         Slack Rake 2/24

Gains Calver Duties 10/24
         Whalf 7/24
         Old Ben 24/24
         Orchard 12/24
         Cowclose Sough 5/24, 1/192
         Broad Meadow 2/24
         Breach Side Sough 2/24
         Froggatt Grove 2/24

Calver Sough 3/24
Bradwell Sough 16/24
Bage 1/48
C.T. 1/72
Flints & Jackson 1/24, 1/48, 1/96
Twenty Lands 12/24
Venture 1/24, 1/48
Gregorys 4/24

This limited evidence on size of shareholding shows very little overlap between the major shareholders and the small investors, which means that an individual with a large proportion of the shares in one sough was unlikely to have a small shareholding in another, and vice-versa.

Shares and values of interests in mines and soughs of Messrs Twigg & Co. 1789 illustrates tendency (probably typical) to have larger holdings in cheaper soughs and small holdings in more expensive soughs. The value of a one-twenty-fourth share is given, hence it is possible to calculate not only Twigg's total investments but also total investment in each of the mines and soughs mentioned.

Mine/sough	Share	Value of 1/24th share £	Value of Twigg's holding £	s	d
Gregorys	1/48	600	300		
Cockwell	1/12	650	1,300		
Pottway	5/24		2,250		
	1/48	450	225		
	1/192		56	10	
Yatestoop sough	5/24		600		
	1/32	120	90		
	1/192		15		
	1/384		7	10	
Placket	7/24	50	350		
	1/48		25		
Drake	3/24		240		
	1/96	80	20		
	1/192		10		
Wills Founder	7/24	20	140		

Mine/sough	Share	Value of 1/24th share £	Value of Twigg's holding £		s	d
Davis	9/24	10	90			
Cowclose	2/24	5	10			
	1/48		2		10	
Stoke sough	2/24	25	50			
	1/192		3		2	6
Wheels rake	12/24	25	300			
Cross Flatts	4/24	5	20			
Cromford Moor Sough	2/24	25	50			
	1/284		1		11	2
Little Brookhead Sough	1/48	20	10			
Little Pasture Sough	2/24	150	300			
	1/384		9		7	6
	1/768		4		13	6
Ladywash Sough	2/24	50	100			
	1/32		37		10	
Haycliffe Sough	1/24	50	50			
Milnes and Middleton Sough	2/24	10	20			
	1/192		1		5	
	1/384				12	6
	1/768				6	2
Dusty Pitts	1/24	10	10			
Moorwoods Sough	1/4	25	150			
	1/48		12		10	
Bradshaws	1/24	10	10			
	1/72		3		6	8
	1/96		2		10	
	1/384				12	6
Watergrove Sough	1/36	300	200			
	1/96		75			
Kackle Mackle	13/24	10	135	13		
Never Fear	12/24	5	60			

Mine/sough	Share	Value of 1/24th share £	Value of Twigg's holding £ s d
Nether Pitts	7/24	5	35
	1/26		3 6 8
Busks	1/24	22	22
	1/96		5 10
	Grand total		£7,415 2 6

These data illustrate the wide variation in investments in mines and soughs, e.g. largest: Cockwell Sough, £15,600; smallest mine: Cowclose, £120. The investment (in 1789) in the soughs in which we are interested:

Cockwell	£15,600
Haycliffe	1,200
Ladywash	1,200
Little Pasture	3,600
Stoke	600
Watergrove	7,200
Bradshaws	240
Moorwoods	600
Cromford Moor	600
Little Brookhead	480
Yatestoop	2,880

From this limited information it is possible to calculate the minimum likely shareholding. For example, Hambleton and Wortley each had 1/96 share in Brookhead (£480), hence their investment was £5 each. It is also possible to see smaller investments, such as 1/192 share in a £240 sough (Bradshaws), which would be 25s, an amount within the reach of a thrifty working man. At the other end of the scale are John Spencer, whose investments in the 1780s totalled over £5,000, and Twigg (£7,415), amounts which would have enabled them to establish themselves in cotton spinning on a large scale.

Although there were very many small investors, there were also some middlesized shareholders such as those who held a 1/24 share in three soughs on Eyam Great Vein (medium-sized). Working on this principle:

1/24 share in Little Pasture	£150
1/24 share in Ladywash	50
1/24 share in Haycliffe	50
Total	£250

These amounts wold have enabled the shareholder to establish himself as a middle-sized brewer.

APPENDIX II

Samuel Crompton's 1811 census of mule spindles sixty miles around Manchester (source: Crompton's papers in the Irving Bequest, Bolton Civic Centre Museum)

	Mule spindles	Throstle spindles
1 (a) Oldham		
Ashton Mill	8,000	
Ashton, the late	7,000	
Bailies	7,000	
Broadhead	8,000	
Coopers	10,400	
Clegg, William	1,920	
Gledhill, James	6,000	
Jackson	3,000	
Jones	7,000	
Lees, Daniel	10,616	
Lees, James	8,000	
Lees, John	11,000	
Lees & Co.	10,000	
Rowland, Joseph	4,000	
Row (Wroe) and Duncuft	1,000	
Taylor & Co.	8,000	
Twemlows	6,000	
Wareings	7,000	
Whittaker, Robert	3,840	
Total, nineteen firms	127,876	
(b) Lees, near Oldham		
Bradock	3,600	
Dronfield	4,320	

	Mule spindles	Throstle spindles
Knott	2,400	
Lees (Barr Mill)	3,600	
Moss	4,320	
Stanfields	1,920	
Sevill	3,600	
Wareings	2,880	
Waterhead Mill	5,760	
In Newton Wood	7,200	
In Newton Wood	14,400	
In Newton Wood	5,280	
Lees total, thirteen firms	63,600	
2 Bolton		
Ainsworth, Thomas & Co.	—	1,000
Ashworth, John & Co.	5,084	
Best	2,252	
Bollings	13,822	
Carliles	22,850	2,576
Chewmoor	1,634	1,004
Chowbent	7,500	1,000
Delf H.	20,000	
Dore Bank	3,640	
Eagly Mill	5,680	
Grimes	3,756	
Grays	8,214	
Gregory & Co.	10,370	
Halls (Quarlton)	3,280	
Horrocks's (Turton)	8,950	
Jones's (New Acres Mill)	5,882	
J. & J. Crook	5,350	1,376
Knotts	9,360	
Know Mill	2,292	
Kershaw and Sudren	5,096	
Lords	10,440	
Lums	10,824	4,760
Makinson, T. & D.	12,520	

	Mule spindles	*Throstle spindles*
Ormrod and Hardcastle	39,210	
Pickering and Platt	6,716	
Prestolees	21,896	
Roger Holland	30,980	
Salt Pye	2,388	
Scrowcrofts B.C.	2,600	
Thomasson (Edgworth)	4,000	
Wood, John & Co.	6,700	
Wylde, Smith & Co.	7,308	
Westleigh	6,137	288
Total, thirty-three firms	306,770	12,004

BIBLIOGRAPHY

Detailed illustration of the relationship between these sources and the individuals of the study can be found in the appendices of my Ph.D. thesis.

Lead

I. *Manuscript sources*

Chatsworth House

Duke of Devonshire's papers

Derby Public Library, Archives Department

Borough deeds
Deeds (various)
Fair book
T. N. Ince pedigrees
St Alkmund's Parish records
Tilley notes
Toft collection
Woolley mss (microfilm)
Wyatt letters

Derbyshire Record Office

Brooke-Taylor papers
Gell Family papers
Hurt Family collection
Stone Symonds collection
Woolley mss
Wyatt papers

John Rylands Library

Bagshaw collection

Lichfield Joint Record Office

Bishop's transcripts of Derbyshire parish registers

Probate inventories
Wills

Sheffield City Library, Archives Department

Bagshaw collection
Barker collection
Crewe muniments
Oakes deeds
Raistrick collection
Spencer Stanhope muniments
Wager Holmes collection

University of Nottingham Library

1851 census (microfilm)

II. *Printed manuscript source*

P. H. Blagg, W. P. W. Philimore and L. L. Simpson (eds.), *Derbyshire Parish Registers: Marriages*, 1935

III. *Newspapers*

Derby Mercury, Derby Reporter

IV. *Directories*

1781. W. Bailey, *Northern Directory*
1826, 1827, 1828, 1829. S. Glover, *The Directory of the County of Derby*
1842. Pigot & Co., *The Directory of Derbyshire*
1846. S. Bagshaw, *The History, Gazetteer and Directory of Derbyshire*
1850. I. Slater, *The Derbyshire Directory for 1850*
1857. F. White, *The History, Gazetteer, and Directory of the County of Derby*
1895. T. Bulmer & Co., *The History, Topography, and Directory of Derbyshire*

V. *Unpublished theses*

R. Burt, 'The Lead Industry of England and Wales, 1700–1880', Ph.D. thesis, University of London, 1971

R. Gould, 'A Study of the Capital formation and Working Conditions in the Wirksworth Lead Mines, 1700–1900', B.A. dissertation, University of Nottingham, 1975

F. S. Ottery, 'The Development of Wirksworth 1800–1965', M.A. thesis,

University of Nottingham, 1965

VI. *Books*

W. Bray, *Sketch of a Tour into Derbyshire and Yorkshire*, London, 1783

J. Britton and E. W. Brayley, *Topography and Historical Description of Derbyshire*, London, 1810

B. Bryan, *Matlock Manor and Parish*, London, 1903

S. D. Chapman, *The Early Factory Masters*, Newton Abbot, 1967

D. Defoe, *A Tour through the whole Island of Great Britain*, London, 1753

K. C. Edwards, *The Peak District*, London, 1962

S. Evans, *Bradwell: Ancient and Modern*, Chesterfield, 1912

T. D. Ford and J. H. Rieuwerts (eds.), *Lead Mining in the Peak District*, Bakewell, 1968

S. Glover, *The Peak Guide*, Derby, 1830

—— *The History and Gazetteer of the County of Derby*, vols. 1 and 2, Derby, 1830

R. R. Hackett, *Wirksworth and Five Miles Around*, Derby, 1899

H. Harris, *Industrial Archaeology of the Peak District*, Newton Abbot, 1971

K. Hudson, *Industrial Archaeology*, London, 1964

N. Kirkham, *Derbyshire Lead Mining*, Truro, 1968

B. R. Mitchell and P. Deane, *Abstract of British Historical Statistics*, Cambridge, 1962

F. Nixon, *Industrial Archaeology of Derbyshire*, Newton Abbot, 1969

J. Pilkington, *A View of the Present State of Derbyshire*, vol. 1, Derby, 1789

A. Raistrick, *Industrial Archaeology. An Historical Survey*, London, 1972

A. Raistrick and B. Jennings, *Lead Mining in the Pennines*, London, 1965

J. Rhodes, *Lead Mining in Derbyshire in the Eighteenth Century*, Sheffield, 1973

J. H. Rieuwerts, *Derbyshire Old Lead Mines and Miners*, Leek, 1972.

——, *Lathkilldale: its Mines and Miners*, Leek, 1973

D. M. Smith, *The Industrial Archaeology of the East Midlands*, Newton Abbot, 1965

Victoria County History of Derby, London, 1907

W. Wood, *The History and Antiquities of Eyam*, Derby, 1865

W. Woolley, *The History of the County of Derby*, Derby, 1712

G. T. Wright, *Longstone Records*, Bakewell, 1906

VII. *Articles*

R. Burt and M. Atkinson, 'The mineral statistics and Derbyshire lead mining', *Bulletin of the Peak District Mines Historical Society*, (hereafter

B.P.D.M.H.S.), VI, No. 3, 1976

R. Burt, 'Lead production in England and Wales, 1700–1770', *Economic History Review*, XXII, 1969

R. Flindall, 'Lead mining in Cromford liberty 1698–1714', *B.P.D.M.H.S.*, V, No. 5, 1974

——, 'A survey of a mine in Tearsall Routh, Wensley', *B.P.D.M.H.S.*, V, No. 6, 1974

R. Flindall and A. Hayes, 'Some early techniques used in the Derbyshire lead mines', *B.P.D.M.H.S.*, VI, No. 2, 1975

J. M. Fuller, 'Lead mining in Derbyshire in mid-nineteenth century', *East Midlands Geographer*, III, Pt 7, No. 23, 1965

G. G. Hopkinson, 'Five generations of Derbyshire lead mining and smelting, 1729–1858', *Derbyshire Archaeological Journal*, LXXVIII, 1958

——, 'Lead mining in eighteenth century Ashover', *Derbyshire Archaeological Journal*, LXXII, 1952

N. Kirkham, 'Ball Eye mine and sough, Cromford', *B.P.D.M.H.S.*, III, No. 3, 1967

——, 'The draining of Wirksworth lead mines', *Derbyshire Archaeological Journal*, reprint, 1960

——, 'Eyam Edge mines and soughs part 1', *B.P.D.M.H.S.*, II, No. 5, 1965

——, 'Eyam Edge mines and soughs part 2', *B.P.D.M.H.S.*, II, No. 6, 1965

——, 'Eyam Edge mines and soughs part 3', *B.P.D.M.H.S.*, III, No. 1, 1966

——, 'Eyam Edge mines and soughs part 4', *B.P.D.M.H.S.*, III, No. 2, 1966

——, 'Great Hucklow mines', *B.P.D.M.H.S.*, II, No. 1, 1963

——, 'Lead mines and Royalists', *Derbyshire Miscellany*, II, No. 5, 1961

——, 'Oakenedge, Streaks and Watergrove soughs', *B.P.D.M.H.S.*, III, No. 4, 1967

——, 'Old Mill Close lead mines', *B.P.D.M.H.S.*, II, No. 2, 1963

——, 'Soughs in Middleton Dale part 1', *B.P.D.M.H.S.*, III, No. 6, 1968

——, 'Tearsall and Dale Field soughs, Wensley', *B.P.D.M.H.S.*, I, No. 6, 1962

——, 'The tumultuous course of Dovegang', *Derbyshire Archaeological Journal*, LXXIII, 1953

——, 'Whale sough and Hubberdale mine', *B.P.D.M.H.S.*, II, No. 4,

1964

——, 'Wheels rake, Alport-by-Youlgreave', *B.P.D.M.H.S.*, II, No. 3, 1964

——, 'Winster sough', *B.P.D.M.H.S.*, I, No. 5, 1961

——, 'Yatestoop sough', *B.P.D.M.H.S.*, I, No. 7, 1962

F. S. Ottery, 'Lead mining in the Wirksworth district during the late eighteenth and early nineteenth century', *B.P.D.M.H.S.*, IV, No. 2, 1969

J. H. Rieuwerts, 'The mines of Calver, Coombs Dale and Longstone Edge', *B.P.D.M.H.S.*, I, No. 3, 1963

——, 'The lead mines and soughs of Eyam Edge', *B.P.D.M.H.S.*, I, No. 3, 1960

——, 'A list of the soughs of the Derbyshire lead mines', *B.P.D.M.H.S.*, III, No. 1, 1966

——, 'The soughs of the Derbyshire lead mines – a supplementary list', *B.P.D.M.H.S.*, IV, No. 2, 1969

J. A. Robey, 'The mines north west of Monyash' *D.M.H.S.*, II, No. 1, 1963

M. E. Smith, 'The Watergrove mine', *B.P.D.M.H.S.*, I, No. 2, 1960

A. H. Stokes 'Lead and lead mining in Derbyshire', *Transactions of the Chesterfield nd Derbyshire Institute of Mining, Civil and Mechanical Engineers*, X, XI and XII, 1881–83

R. Thornhill, 'Some accounts of an eighteenth century lead mining agent in Great Longstone, 1776–1827', *B.P.D.M.H.S.*, III, No. 4, 1967

H. Thorpe, 'Derbyshire lead production', *Derbyshire Countryside*, III, 1934

A. E. Wiles, 'The north side of Ashford lordship 1750–1850, *B.P.D.M.H.S.*, II, No. 1, 1963

C. J. Williams and L. Willies, 'Stone Edge cupola', *B.P.D.M.H.S.*, III, No. 1, 1968

L. Willies, 'Cupola lead smelting sites in Derbyshire 1737–1900', *B.P.D.M.H.S.*, IV, No. 1, 1969

——, 'Gabriel Jars (1732–1769) and the Derbyshire lead industry', *B.P.D.M.H.S.*, V, No. 1, 1972

——, 'A note on the price of lead 1730–1900', *B.P.D.M.H.S.*, V, No. 1, 1972

——, 'Winster and eighteenth century lead mining', *B.P.D.M.H.S.*, III, No. 5, 1968

Cotton

I. *Manuscript sources*
(a) *1787*

Lancashire Record Office

>   Cavendish of Holker papers (DDCa)
>   Land Tax Returns–Lancashire, 1780–1832 (QDL)
>   Miscellaneous papers (DDX)

Manchester Central Library Archives Department

>   Assessment of Factories, Houses, Shops and Warehouses (ms M9/40/1/20)
>   Records of Samuel Gregg's Mills at Quarry Bank, Styal, 1/84–1900
>   Schedule of Deeds (ms M/c 1120–1159)
>   J. Schole, 'Foreign Merchants Guide for 1784'
>   Spinners Memorial, July 1810 (ms M3/3/7)

West Yorkshire County Record Office, Wakefield

>   Deeds

(b) *1811*

Bolton Central Museum and Library

>   Crompton mss
>   Land surveys and valuations
>   Papers of William Gray & Sons
>   Papers of Thomas Pilkington
>   Poor Relief assessment books, 1770–1821
>   Thompson collection

Lancashire Record Office

>   Cavendish of Holker papers (DDCa)
>   The *Lancashire Evening Post* deposits (DDPr)
>   Land Tax Returns – Lancashire, 1780–1832 (QDL)
>   Miscellaneous papers (DDX)
>   Papers deposited by N. G. Rees of Oldham (DDRe)
>   Scarisbrick of Scarisbrick papers (DDSc)

Oldham Public Library, Archives Department

>   Butterworth mss

G. Higson mss
Giles Shaw mss

Wigan Reference Library

Miscellaneous mss

Williams & Glyns Bank, St Ann's Square, Manchester

Heywood Brothers (Bankers), ledgers, 1795–96

II. *Printed manuscript sources*
1787
P. H. Blagg, L. L. Simpson and A. P. Wadsworth (eds.), *Nottinghamshire Parish Registers: Marriages.*
J. T. Godfrey (ed.), *The Stretton MSS*

III. *British Parliamentary Papers*
The Returns of Cotton and other Mills, 1803–04
Reports from the Select Committee on Manufacturers, Commerce and Shipping, 1833
Factories Inquiry Commission, 1833

IV. *Newspapers*
(*a*) 1787: *Leeds Mercury, Manchester Mercury.*
(*b*) 1811: *Daily Dispatch, Oldham Chronicle, Oldham Evening Chronicle.*

V. *Directories*
1772. E. Raffald, *The Manchester Directory for the year 1772*
1773. E. Raffald, *The Manchester Directory for the year 1773*
1781. E. Raffald, *The Manchester Directory for the year 1781*
1781, 1783. W. Bailey, *Northern Directory*
1787. W. Tunnicliffe, *A Topographical Survey of the Counties of Stafford, Chester and Lancaster*
1788. E. Holme, *A Directory for the towns of Manchester and Salford for the year 1788*
1790. *Universal British Directory of Trade, Commerce and Manufacture*
1794. Scholes. *Manchester and Salford Directory*
1797. J. Ryley, *The Leeds Directory*
1800. Binns and Brown, *A Directory for the Town of Leeds*
1804, 1808, 1809. Dean & Co., *Manchester and Salford Directory*
1805. Holden, *Triennial Directory for Bolton*

1806. *Commercial Directory for Bolton*
1811. Dean, *Manchester and Salford Directory*
1813. Pigot & Co., *Manchester and Salford Directory*
1815, 1817, 1819–20. Pigot and Dean, *Manchester and Salford Directory*
1843. I. Slater, *A Directory of Manchester and Salford and the Townships Contiguous*
1845. I. Slater, *A General and Classified Directory and Street Register of Manchester and Salford and their Vicinities*
1846. S. Bagshaw, *History, Gazetteer, and Directory of Derbyshire*

VI. *Unpublished theses*
J. A. Fox, 'The Social Origins, Careers and Characteristics of Entrepreneurs in South Lancashire during the Nineteenth Century', M.A. dissertation, University of Lancaster, 1970
V.A.C. Gattrell, 'The Commercial Middle Class in Manchester, c. 1820–1857', Ph.D. thesis, University of Cambridge, 1971
G. Ingle, 'A History of R. V. Marriner Ltd, Worsted Spinners, Keighley', M.Phil. thesis, University of Leeds, 1974
W. Lazenby, 'The Social and Economic History of Styal', M.A. thesis, University of Manchester, 1949
G. Shutt, 'Wharfedale Water Mills', M.Phil. thesis, University of Leeds, 1979

VII. *Books*
W. A. Abram, *A History of Blackburn Town and Parish*, London, 1877
J. Aiken, *A Description of the Country from Thirty to Forty Miles around Manchester*, London, 1795
O. Ashmore, *The Industrial Archaeology of Lancashire*, Newton Abbot, 1969
C. Aspin and S. D. Chapman, *James Hargreaves and the Spinning Jenny*, Preston, 1964
C. Aspin (ed.), *Reach's Manchester and the Textile District in 1846*, Helmshore, 1972
R. S. Atwood, *The Localisation of the Cotton Industry in Lancashire, England*, Florida, 1930
E. Baines, *A History of the Cotton Manufacture in Great Britain*, London, 1835
B. T. Barton, *Historical Gleanings of Bolton and District*, vols. I and II, Bolton, 1881
H. Bateson, *A Century History of Oldham*, Oldham, 1949

R. Boyson, *The Ashworth Cotton Enterprise*, Oxford, 1970

J. Brierley, *Borough of Oldham. Jubilee of Incorporation*, Oldham, 1899

J. D. Briscoe, *A Hand-book of the History and Topography of Bolton*, Bolton, 1861

W. E. Brown, *Robert Heywood of Bolton 1786–1868*, Wakefield, 1970

J. Butt (ed.), *Robert Owen: Prince of Cotton Spinners*, Newton Abbot, 1971

E. Butterworth, *Historical Sketches of Oldham*, Oldham, 1856

——, *A Statistical Sketch of the County Palatine of Lancaster*, Oldham, 1841

J. Butterworth, *A Complete History of the Trades of Manchester*, Manchester, 1822

——, *History and Description of the Parochial Chapelry of Oldham*, Oldham, 1826

H. Cameron, *Samuel Crompton*, London, 1950

H. Catling, *The Spinning Mule*, Newton Abbot, 1970

S. D. Chapman, *The Cotton Industry in the Industrial Revolution*, London, 1972

——, *The Early Factory Masters*, Newton Abbot, 1967

S. J. Chapman, *The Lancashire Cotton Industry*, Manchester, 1904

J. Clegg, *Annals of Bolton*, Bolton, 1888

F. Collier and R. S. Fitton, *The Family Economy of the Working Classes in the Cotton Industry*, Chetham Society, XII, Manchester, 1965

P. Colquhoun, *An Important Crisis in the Cotton Manufactory Explained*, London, 1788

P. L. Cottrell, *Industrial Finance 1830–1914*, London, 1980

W. B. Crump, *The Leeds Woollen Industry 1780–1820*, Leeds, 1931

W. B. Crump and G. Ghorbal, *A History of the Huddersfield Woollen Industry*, Huddersfield, 1935

G. W. Daniels, *The Early English Cotton Industry*, Manchester, 1920

C. S. Davies (ed.), *A History of Macclesfield*, Manchester, 1961

W. H. Dawson, *A History of Skipton*, Skipton, 1882

M. M. Edwards, *The Growth of the British Cotton Trade, 1780–1815*, Manchester, 1967

W. English, *The Textile Industry*, London, 1969

J. Farey, *Agriculture of Derbyshire*, vol. II, London, 1811–17

R. S. Fitton and A. P. Wadsworth, *The Strutts and the Arkwrights, 1758–1830*, Manchester, 1958

J. Foster, *Class Struggle and the Industrial Revolution: Early Industrial Capitalism in Three English Towns*, London, 1974

G. J. French, *The Life and Times of Samuel Crompton*, first edition 1869, reprinted Bath, 1970

H. S. Gibb, *Autobiography of a Manchester Cotton Manufacturer*, Manchester, 1887

G. P. Gore, *Oldham Chapelry*, Oldham, 1906

Mrs Hall, *Memoirs of Marshall Hall by his Widow*, London, 1861

H. Hamilton, *An Economic History of Scotland in the Eighteenth Century*, Oxford, 1963

J. Hodgson, *Textile Manufacture and other Industries in Keighley*, Keighley, 1879

E. Hopwood, *A History of the Lancashire Cotton Industry and the Amalgamated Weavers Association*, Manchester, 1969

J. Kennedy, *Miscellaneous Papers*, Manchester, 1849

——, *On the Rise and Progress of the Cotton Trade*, Manchester, 1849

G. H. Lee, *A Cotton Enterprise 1795–1840. A History of M'Connel and Kennedy, Fine Cotton Spinners*, Manchester, 1972

J. D. Marshall, *Furness and the Industrial Revolution. An Economic History of Furness*, Barrow, 1958

P. Mathias, *The Transformation of England*, London, 1979

F. Mills, *Oldham Master Cotton Spinners Association Ltd. Centenary 1866–1966*, Oldham, 1966

J. Montgomery, *The Theory and Practice of Cotton Spinning*, Glasgow, 1833

J. Mortimer, *Industrial Lancashire. Some Manufacturing Towns and their Surroundings*, Manchester, 1896

S. Pigott, *Hollins. A Study of Industry 1784–1949*, Nottingham, 1949

J. C. Scholes, *History of Bolton*, Bolton, 1892

S. Shapiro, *Capital and the Cotton Industry in the Industrial Revolution*, New York, 1967

G. Shaw, *Annals of Oldham 1731–1783*, vol. 2, Oldham, 1905

—— (ed.), *Oldham, Local Notes and Gleanings*, vols. 1, 2 and 3, Oldham, 1887–89

S. Shaw, *The History and Antiquities of Staffordshire*, vols. 1 and 2, London, 1798–1801

W. C. Taylor, *Notes of a Tour in the Manufacturing District of Lancashire*, London, 1842

G. H. Tupling, *The Economic History of Rossendale*, Chetham Society, LXXXVI, Manchester, 1927

G. Turnbull, *A History of the Calico Printing Industry of Great Britain*, Altrincham, 1951

A. Ure, *The Cotton Manufacture of Great Britain Investigated and Illustrated*, vols. 1 and 2, London, 1861

A. P. Wadsworth and J. de L. Mann, *The Cotton Trade and Industrial Lancashire, 1600–1780*, Manchester, 1931

F. A. Wells, *Hollins and Viyella. A Study in Business History*, Newton Abbot, 1968

P. A. Whittle, *Bolton-le-Moors*, Bolton, 1855

H. Wilde, *Mills and Mill Owners of the Last Century*, Oldham, 1934

VII. *Articles*

O. Ashmore, 'Low Moor, Clitheroe: a nineteenth century factory community', *Transactions of the Lancashire and Cheshire Antiquarian Society*, LXXIII and LXXIV, 1963–64

C. Aspin, 'New evidence on James Hargreaves and the spinning jenny', *Textile History*, I, 1968

J. Brown, 'A memoir of Robert Blincoe', *Derbyshire Archaeological Society, Local History Section*, Supplement X 1966

W. H. Chaloner, 'The Cheshire activities of Matthew Boulton and James Watt, of Soho, near Birmingham, 1776–1817', *Transactions of the Lancashire and Cheshire Antiquarian Society*, LXI, 1949

——, 'Robert Owen, Peter Drinkwater and the early factory system in Manchester, 1788–1800', *Bulletin of the John Rylands Library*, XXXVII, 1955

——, 'The Stockdale family, the Wilkinson brothers and the cotton mills at Cark-in-Cartmel, *c.* 1782–1850', *Transactions of the Cumberland and Westmorland Antiquarian and Archaeological Society*, LXIV, 1964

S. D. Chapman, 'Financial restraints on the growth of firms in the cotton industry, 1790–1850', *Economic History Review*, XXXII, 1979

——, 'Fixed capital formation in the British cotton industry, 1770–1815', *Economic History Review*, XXIII, 1970

——, 'James Longsdon, 1745–1821, farmer and fustian manufacturer: the small firm in the early English cotton industry', *Textile History*, I, 1968

——, 'The Peels in the early English cotton industry', *Business History*, XI, 1969

——, 'Pioneers of worsted spinning by power', *Business History*, VII, 1965

——, 'Sutton old mill', *Journal of Industrial Archaeology*, II, 1965

——, 'The transition to the factory system in the Midlands cotton spinning industry', *Economic History Review*, XVI, 1965

F. Collier, 'Samuel Gregg and Styal Mill', *Memoirs and Proceedings of the Manchester Literary and Philosophical Society*, LXXXV, 1941–43

G. W. Daniels, 'Crompton's census of the cotton industry in 1811', *Economic History*, II, 1930–33

E. J. Foulkes, 'The cotton spinning factories of Flintshire, 1777–1866', *Flintshire Historical Society Publications*, XXI, 1964

V. A. C. Gatrell, 'Labour, power and the size of firms in Lancashire cotton in the second quarter of the nineteenth century', *Economic History Review*, XXX, 1977

B. Hadfield, 'The Carrs silk mills, Stockport', *The Manchester School*, V, No. 2, 1934

J. Lindsay, 'An early industrial community: the Evans' cotton mill at Darley Abbey, Derbyshire, 1783–1810', *Business History Review*, XXXIV, 1960

R. Lloyd-Jones and A. A. Le Roux, 'The size of firms in the cotton industry: Manchester, 1815–41', *Economic History Review*, XXXIII, 1980

J. D. Marshall, 'Early application of stream power: the cotton mills of the Upper Lean', *Transactions of the Thoroton Society of Nottinghamshire*, LX, 1956

M. H. Mackenzie, 'The Bakewell cotton mill and the Arkwrights', *Derbyshire Archaeological Journal*, LXXIX, 1959

——, 'Calver Mill and its owners', *Derbyshire Archaeological Journal*, LXXXIII and LXXXIV, 1963–4

H. W. Ogden, 'The geographical basis of the Lancashire cotton industry', *Journal of the Textile Institute*, XVIII, 1927

A. Parker, 'The Nottingham potters', *Transactions of the Thoroton Society*, XXXVI, 1932

M. Rose, 'Samuel Crompton, 1753–1827, inventor of the spinning mule: a reconsideration', *Transactions of the Lancashire and Cheshire Antiquarian Society*, LXXV and LXXVI, 1965–66

E. M. Sigsworth, 'William Greenwood and Robert Heaton: two eighteenth century worsted manufacturers', *Journal of the Bradford Textile Society*, 1951–52

J. Sleigh, 'The old Ashbourne families', *Derbyshire Archaeological Journal*, III, 1881

Lace

I. *Manuscript sources*
Nottingham City Library Archives Department

Assessment Book of Highways, 1801

Corporation archives
Deeds of property
Nottingham registers of apprentices
Nottingham Watch and Ward lists
Partnership agreements
Rate collection books, 1796–1807
Restriction deeds (petition of lace machine holders in 1829)
Wills

Nottinghamshire Record Office

Nottingham marriage registers for: St Mary's, St Nicholas's, and St Peter's parishes, Nottingham; Basford, Beeston, Carlton, Radford, Sneinton

Public Record Office

Chancery Exhibits (J90/779)

University of Nottingham Library

1851 census returns for Nottinghamshire (microfilm)

II. *British Parliamentary Papers*
Factory Enquiry Commission: First Report of the Central Board, 1833
Second Report on Employment of Children in Factories, and Supplementary Report, part 1, 1833; *Supplementary Report*, 1834
Report on the Sanitary Condition of Nottingham from the Report from the Commissioners to Enquire into the State of large Towns, 1845

III. *Newspapers*
Nottingham Evening Post; Nottingham Journal, 1820–40; *Nottingham Review*, 1820–40; *Nottinghamshire Weekly Guardian*

IV. *Directories*
1818. *Triennial Directory for the Town of Nottingham*
1825. S. Glover, *Nottingham Directory*
1834. W. Dearden, *History, Topography and Directory of the Town of Nottingham*
1839. Pigot & Co., *Directory of Nottinghamshire*
1840. J. Orange, *The Nottingham Annual Register and Directory*
1843. *Directory of Nottingham*
1844. S. Glover, *History and Directory for the Town and County of Nottingham*

1848. Lascelles and Hagar, *Commercial Directory*
1854. Wright & Co., *Nottingham Directory and Borough Register*

V. *Nottingham poll books*
1818, 1820, 1826. *A List of Burgesses and Freeholders*
1832. *A List of Burgesses, Freeholders and Householders*
1841. *A List of Burgesses, Occupiers and Freeholders*

VI. *Unpublished theses*
S. D. Chapman, 'William Felkin, 1795–1874', M.A. thesis, University of Nottingham, 1960
R. A. Church, 'The Social and Economic Development of Nottingham', Ph.D. thesis, University of Nottingham, 1960

VII. *Books*
W. G. Allen, *John Heathcoat and his Heritage*, London, 1958
J. Blackner, *A History of Nottingham*, Nottingham, 1815
C. Brown, *Lives of Nottinghamshire Worthies*, London, 1882
C. H. Chalklin, *The Provincial Towns of Georgian England: a Study of the Building Phases*, London, 1974
J. D. Chambers, *A Century of Nottingham History 1851–1951*, Nottingham, 1952
C. C. Channer and M. E. Roberts, *Lace Making in the Midlands, Past and Present*, London, 1900
N. H. Cuthbert, *The Lace Makers' Society*, Nottingham, 1960
H. Field, *Nottingham Date Book 1750–1879*, Nottingham, 1880
W. Felkin, *A History of the Machine Wrought Hosiery and Lace Manufactures*, London, 1867
S. T. Hall, *Biographical Sketches*, London, 1873
Z. Halls, *Machine Made Lace in Nottingham in the Eighteenth and Nineteenth Centuries*, Nottingham, 1973
J. L. and B. Hammond, *The Skilled Labourer, 1760–1832*, London, 1930
G. Henson, *A History of the Framework Knitters*, 1831
R. Mellors, *In and about Nottinghamshire*, Nottingham, 1908
——, *Old Nottingham Suburbs, Then and Now*, Nottingham, 1914
——, *Local Papers*, Nottingham, 1916
——, *Men of Nottingham and Nottinghamshire*, Nottingham, 1924
Nottingham Chamber of Commerce Year Book, Nottingham, 1914
H. A. Silverman (ed.), *Studies in Industrial Organisation*, London, 1946
J. F. Sutton, *Date Book of Nottingham, 1750–1850*, Nottingham, 1852

M. I. Thomis (ed.), *Luddism in Nottinghamshire*, London, 1972

D. E. Varley, *A History of the Midland Counties Lace Manufacturers' Association*, Long Eaton, 1959

A. C. Wood, *A History of Nottinghamshire*, Nottingham, 1947

W. H. Wylie, *Nottingham Hand Book*, Nottingham, 1857

———, *Old and New Nottingham*, London and Nottingham, 1853

VIII. *Articles*

'A day at the Nottingham lace manufactories', *Penny Magazine*, 1843

W. B. Carter, 'The lace trade of Nottingham', *Local Preachers Magazine*, January–February, 1880

S. D. Chapman, 'Enterprise and innovation in the British hosiery industry, 1750–1850', *Textile History*, V, 1974

W. Felkin, 'Statistics of the labouring classes and paupers in Nottingham', *Journal of the Royal Statistical Society*, II, 1839

J. E. Heath, 'Lace tenement factory', *Journal of Industrial Archaeology*, XI, 1974

J. D. Marshall, 'The Nottinghamshire reformers and their contribution to the new Poor Law', *Economic History Review*, XIII, 1961

Anon, 'Nottingham lace: its history and manufacture', *Blackwood's Magazine*, CXXIII, 1882

D. E. Varley, 'John Heathcoat, 1783–1861: founder of the machine-made lace industry', *Textile History*, 1, 1968

INDEX

D